Saints Galore

Character
Sketches
for the
New Calendar
of Saints

by David L. Veal

A Forward Movement Maxi Book

It is very meet, right, and our bounden
duty, that we should at all times, and
in all places, give thanks unto thee,
O Lord, Holy Father, Almighty, Everlasting God. Who, in the multitude of
thy Saints, hast compassed us about
with so great a cloud of witnesses that
we, rejoicing in their fellowship, may
run with patience the race that is set
before us, and, together with them, may
receive the crown of glory that fadeth
not away.

The Preface for All Saints Day
Book of Common Prayer

Second Printing

© *1972 Forward Movement Publications*
412 Sycamore Street
Cincinnati, Ohio 45202
50 cents per copy

The Holy Name of our Lord Jesus Christ

The Circumcision and Naming of Jesus

In keeping with ancient Jewish tradition, Jesus was circumcised and named on the eighth day after his birth. The New Israel, the church, no longer requires circumcision and one is tempted to say, "Why all this fuss about a name? What's in a name?"

But names are important symbols. We stencil our names on items that belong to us. Adam named the animals, indicating his lordship over them. Slaves usually assumed the name of the family to which they belonged. A child is named by and for its parents and a bride assumes the name of the family she joins in marriage. Everyone is jealous of the public use of his name and men fear being nameless, "just a number." The third Commandment warns us against taking the Lord's Name in vain.

A name, then, is not just a word, but rather an important sign of ownership and responsibility. In our Lord's family, the church, all that we own or do is in Jesus' Name, "in whom the whole family in heaven and earth is named." Today we remember the naming of Jesus Christ on the occasion of his circumcision. Perhaps this is an appropriate time to dedicate the new year to the greater glory of that Name and all that it stands for.

Plant in every heart, we pray, the love of him who is the Savior of the world.

3

The Epiphany of our Lord Jesus Christ

Christ is Made Known to the World

In the course of time the Lordship of Christ was revealed to various men. The "Wisemen from the East" observed his star and were guided to his cradle where they worshiped him as a newborn king. When John baptised him in the Jordan, the Holy Spirit descended "as a dove" and a voice from heaven proclaimed, "This is my beloved Son in whom I am well pleased." At a wedding feast at Cana his embarrassed host was amazed when Jesus turned water into wine. He revealed himself to his disciples and through their witness the knowledge of him spread. As the church grew, its witness to him was formalized in the sacraments and the canonical scriptures. In the Epiphany season we remember these events and the expanding revelation and manifestation of Christ to the world. We pray for the continuing growth of his kingdom until, "The earth shall be filled with the glory of God as the waters cover the sea."

In the ancient Eastern Church, January 6th was observed as the feast of the Nativity, "Christmas." The Eve of Epiphany is still observed in some places as the "Twelfth Night" of Christmas and the conclusion of the Nativity season.

O God, lead all peoples of the earth to know your only Son now by faith, and in the world to come to see him in the splendor of his glory.

4

William Laud

Died January 10, 1645

Archbishop of Canterbury

Anglican Martyr

William Laud was a humble tailor's son who proved his competence in the Church of England as a scholar and administrator and in 1633 was elected Archbishop of Canterbury. By then the church was seriously weakened by the controversies of the Reformation. Laud attempted to renew the power of the church and to restore its influence over the lives of men. As an advocate of "Uniformity" and the "Via Media" of the Church of England, he encountered violent opposition from various extremist groups. He made powerful enemies when he opposed the brutal practice of "enclosure."

Archbishop Laud was sincere, positive, quite self-less in his devotion to duty, and surprisingly tolerant for his time. He was tragically tactless and undiplomatic and sadly inept at reading public opinion. He was unable to stem the rising tide of Puritan political power in England. The most extreme militants gained control of the government and beheaded Laud on a trumped-up charge of treason. He died with the dignity and confidence of a Christian martyr. Indeed, he is often considered such. All of England was soon to learn how ruthless and tyranical the militant wing of the Puritan party could be.

The Prayer for Congress and the Prayer for the Church might serve as fruitful reading on his feast day since both are Laud's.

Hilary

Bishop of Poitiers

Pastor and Teacher in Gaul

Hilary was born of a powerful pagan family in Gaul. He became a Christian and, perhaps due to the prestige of his name, was elected Bishop of Poitiers as a young, married layman. He accepted the call, "with fear and trembling," and threw himself wholeheartedly into the task of shepherding his flock.

In his time many Christians in Gaul were Arians. That is, they accepted Jesus as "master and son of God," but denied that he was truly God. Hilary questioned the truth of such teaching and was soon exiled by Arian leaders of the church. He fled to the Eastern Mediterranean, then the heartland of Christianity, and there he learned theology and developed his pastoral skills. Tutored by the same Christian leaders who wrote the Nicene Creed, Hilary became a champion of the orthodox Christian faith. He not only returned to his diocese, but he eventually gained general acceptance there and exerted influence throughout Western Europe.

He was a tireless teacher. One of his famous pupils was Martin of Tours (see November 11). Hilary was largely responsible for the acceptance of the Nicene Creed in Western Europe. We honor him best when we seek a genuine understanding of Trinitarian doctrine.

Grant that we may hold fast to your servant Hilary's faith in Jesus Christ as Very God and Very Man.

Antony

Abbot in Egypt

Father of Christian Monasticism

Many young men of the third century world despaired of their decaying, materialistic, and licentious society. In Egypt many fled into the desert in protest and for their own soul's health. Sometimes their behavior became almost as bizarre and unbalanced as the behavior of those from whom they fled. This was not true of Antony.

Antony's quiet and well ordered life of devotion in the desert stood out in contrast both to the wickedness of the contemporary world and the eccentricities of some other hermits. He gave away all his possessions to the poor and thereby freed himself from the demands of property. Still, he found that he had to fight a seemingly endless battle against his personal passions and temptations. He helped fellow Christian hermits to organize their lives in meaningful patterns of prayer, work, and meditation.

His own solitude was frequently interrupted by his concern for the secular church and by requests for counseling. He was a friend to Athanasius (see May 2) and his orthodoxy was unquestionable. It has been said that, "Alone in the desert, Antony stood in the midst of mankind."

Grant that the same Spirit which enabled Antony to withstand the temptations of the world may so strengthen us.

Peter

Strong Fisherman and Apostle

The confession of the disciple Simon Peter, "Thou art the Christ, the Son of the living God," is a milestone in the Lord's ministry, in the founding of the church, and in the history of mankind. On Peter's confession of faith lay the foundation of a new world order.

Peter was a simple fisherman of Gallilee, rough and impetuous. Andrew, his brother, called him to follow Jesus. He soon grew very close and dear to the Lord and was one of the "inner circle" of Jesus' companions. He was quick-tempered and impulsive, given to bursts of enthusiasm and lulls of depression. At the Last Supper he swore he would die rather than forsake Jesus, but he soon denied him thrice.

Following the Resurrection, Peter emerged as leader of the more conservative disciples, strenuously opposing the baptism of Gentiles. However, after a very dramatic dream, he had a real change of heart (see February 4).

Peter eventually went to Rome where, with Paul, he founded the mother church of Western Europe. There, during the Neronian persecutions, he was crucified with his head down. The peculiar position was at his own request for he did not feel worthy to suffer in the same manner as his Lord.

Almighty Father, who inspired Simon Peter, first among the apostles, to confess Jesus as the Messiah and Son of the living God: Keep your Church steadfast upon the rock of this faith.

Wulfstan

Bishop of Worcester

Protector of the Poor and Oppressed

Most students of history are aware of the cruel treatment the native English (Anglo-Saxons) received from their Norman conquerors after 1066. Few know that practically their only effective defender was the English bishop, Wulfstan of Worcester.

Wulfstan was reared by devoted Christian parents and was educated in the church. He entered the priesthood and was soon elected Bishop of Worcester, a position which he declined, prefering to enter a monastery. Some twenty-five years later, in the troubled years just prior to the Norman Conquest, he was again elected to the same bishophric and then accepted the call.

Wulfstan continued to live in virtual poverty. He encouraged laymen to exercise their rights and responsibilities in governing the church. After the Conquest, he did not hesitate to confront the Norman King and the Norman archbishop, appealing to their consciences as Christians and speaking at great personal risk. He secured some rights for the English serfs against their Norman landlords and for English laymen against their Norman bishops. With the help of Archbishop Lanfranc, he succeeded in ending the loathsome practice of selling Englishmen as slaves in Ireland. Wulfstan spent most of his ministry taking the Gospel and the Sacraments to the poor and the oppressed, the English people whom he loved so much.

Fabian

Died January 20, 250

Bishop and Martyr of Rome

Scholar and Leader

In 236 a virtually unknown Christian layman was elected Bishop of Rome. Countless legends have arisen to explain his surprising election. Besides being simply a layman and not a native of Rome, he seems to have carried no outstanding distinction as a scholar or leader. He turned out to be a first-rate bishop in this important diocese. He is reported to have been an efficient organizer and administrator. Not being particularly well trained himself, he corresponded with Origen, Cyprian, and other knowledgeable Christians of Eastern Europe.

For fourteen years he faithfully and effectively guided the church in Rome. He dispatched some of the first missionaries to Gaul. Things seemed to be "coming up roses" for the Roman Church. Then, without warning, a severe persecution of Christians was initiated by a new Emperor, Decius. Bishop Fabian was one of the first to die.

Fabian's life is a bold reminder of how the calls of God and man come upon us unexpectedly, "like a thief in the night." Fabian recognized his call and responded faithfully in his living and in his dying.

O Almighty God, who has called us to faith in you, and has surrounded us with so great a cloud of witnesses: Grant that we, encouraged by the good example of your servant Fabian, may persevere in running the race that is set before us.

Agnes

Martyr at Rome

Youthful Witness

Under orders from the Emperor Diocletian, in 304, the giant politico-military machine of the Roman Empire went to work to rid itself of the troublesome subversives called Christians. Many children were the innocent victims of this efficient blood purge. Agnes of Rome is a famous example.

She was reared a Christian and when the persecution began, although Agnes was but a young teenager, she wished to witness for the faith. A Roman official was attracted to her and might easily have saved her life. He offered her jewerly and many pleasant gifts if she would renounce the Lord and her parents and worship the Roman gods. Infatuated by the innocent girl, the official then attempted to seduce her. She resisted and he became enraged. He had her tortured and publicly stripped and abused. At the culmination of this hideous orgy she was killed with a sword.

The Roman world was stunned by the story of Agnes' suffering, much as our world was stunned by the *Diary of Anne Frank*. In the next generation, when Christianity was made legal, a shrine was erected in her honor in Rome, and the Song of Mary, the Magnificat (Luke 1:46f), was sung in thanksgiving for the witness of little Agnes. God had indeed "put down the mighty from their seat" and "exalted the humble and meek."

Grant that we may share her pure faith in you.

11

Vincent

Died January 22, 304

Deacon of Saragossa and Martyr

Steadfast and Faithful

Vincent was a deacon in an early Christian church in Saragossa, Spain. He was a trusted friend and assistant of the bishop, Valerius. He was a very effective leader and therefore a "prize catch" for the Spanish Governor, Datian, who was implementing the Emperor Diocletian's policy of persecution. Datian's agents used every means known to them to "brainwash" Vincent, since, if he gave up Christianity, it would surely result in the defection of others.

Vincent was submitted to intensive argumentation, interrupted by excruciating tortures. He was beaten, chained, stretched on the rack, cooked on a gridiron, and the floor of his bare cell was covered with broken glass on which he had to walk and recline. Vincent did not renounce Christ or acknowledge the Roman deities.

Finally the exhausted and mutilated saint was released, perhaps as an example to other Christians of what they might have to suffer. He died shortly after his release. But his steadfastness, far from discouraging other Christians, strengthened them in their determination to remain faithful to the Lord.

Even as your holy Deacon and Martyr Vincent triumphed over suffering and despised death: Grant that we may endure hardness and wax valiant in fight.

12

Phillips Brooks

Died January 23, 1893

Bishop of Massachusetts

Renowned Preacher and Pastor

Although many know him only as the author of "O Little Town of Bethlehem," Phillips Brooks was probably the greatest American preacher of the nineteenth century. He was a native of Boston and was educated at Harvard University and the Virginia Seminary. He served two churches in Philadelphia and was for twenty-two years the rector of Trinity Church, Boston. He died less than two years after his election as Bishop of Massachusetts.

We have volumes of his sermons and they are certainly excellent, but reading them today one misses their most important ingredient, the warmth and strength of the person who composed and delivered them. He had a real gift for warming the hearts and stimulating the minds of his listeners. James Bryce wrote, "There was no sign of art about his preaching, no touch of self-consciousness. He spoke to his audience as a man might speak to his friend, pouring forth with swift, yet quiet and seldom impassioned, earnestness the thoughts and feelings of his singularly pure and lofty spirit." He preached sound Christian doctrine to listeners who ostensibly had no interest in such—and he got by with it! Although he was theologically quite orthodox and conservative, he came to be considered a "liberal" leader in his day simply because of his concern and interest in the social and intellectual issues of the times.

Paul

Apostle to the Gentiles

Paul has been called by some modern writers, "the true founder of the church" and even "the first Christian." Although we may reject such statements as exaggerations, they do reflect the enormous importance of this man in the development of our faith and our community in history.

The occasion of Paul's conversion has long been regarded as a major turning point in Christian history. He had been an enthusiastic Jew, a Pharisee, in fact, and had studied under one of the great Rabbis of his day, Gamaliel. He advocated and witnessed the stoning of Stephen (see December 26) and was enroute to Damascus to assist in the further persecution of the Christians there when his dramatic conversion took place.

From then on his life was totally devoted to the service of Christ, and especially to the conversion of non-Jewish people. His letters and the Book of Acts give us a wealth of information regarding his life and work. He founded churches in Philippi, Athens, Thessalonica, Corinth, and many other important cities of his day. He is generally believed to have died with Peter in Rome, a victim of the persecution of Nero.

O God, grant that we may hold in remembrance your apostle Paul's wonderful conversion, and show our thanksgiving by following his holy teaching.

14

Timothy and Titus

Companions of Saint Paul

Both Timothy and Titus were gentiles, i.e. non-Jews, converted by Paul. Each seems to have accepted the Christian faith at the end of a long and deep personal struggle. It was not an easy step to take. Nor did the early church find it easy to accept a gentile into the "household of the faithful" (see February 4).

These men became close friends of Paul, and they accompanied him on several of his missionary journeys where they proved to be invaluable assistants, especially in the Greek cities of Corinth and Thessalonica.

From Paul's letter to Titus, which is contained in the New Testament, we assume that the Apostle left Titus on the island of Crete. Titus is believed to have been the chief organizer of the church on that island.

Paul frequently used Timothy as a "trouble-shooter" and "follow-up man" in his ministry. Timothy followed Paul to Rome and visited him in prison there, but escaped the Neronian persecution. Timothy spent his last days witnessing to Christ in Ephesus where, according to Eusebius, he was beaten to death by a mob of pagans among whom he had opposed the licentious festivities of the goddess Diana.

Almighty and merciful God, who called your servants Timothy and Titus to endure hardship for the sake of your dear Son: Strengthen us in like manner to stand firm in adversity.

John Chrysostom

Died January 27, 407

Bishop of Constantinople

Great Preacher and Pastor

In an influential, prosperous, and sophisticated city at the apex of international power, it is rarely popular to advocate restraint, self-control, and responsible living. When the leaders of mighty Constantinople elected John Chrysostom to be Patriarch of the city they thought they had elected a "holy man" who would bless and affirm them in their way of living. They were only half right.

Bishop John's powerful sermons in the great cathedral, Santa (Hagia) Sophia, soon became a "cauldron of scalding water" thrown in the faces of the rich and proud citizens of Constantinople. His example of piety, charity, and simple living was an embarrassment to many. Eventually, through the intrigue of a vain and powerful lady, Eudoxia, and a jealous and corrupt clergyman, Theophilus, John was exiled. He died as a prisoner on a forced march into the Caucasus Mountains in winter, a martyr for righteousness in a society bent on lust. However, his preaching and exemplary living had so touched the hearts of many that sweeping reforms were soon instituted and life in the great city was profoundly changed for a generation or more.

The numerous volumes which we have of his sermons and commentaries have not lost their relevance today. The Liturgy of the Church in Constantinople, which he profoundly influenced, still bears his name. From this we get the "Prayer of St. Chrysostom" (Prayer Book, page 20).

Thomas Aquinas
Friar

Died January 28, 1274

Famous Theologian

Perhaps the greatest of the many medieval theologians, Thomas was the son of a prominent Italian count. He joined the Dominican Order against the will of his family. He studied at Monte Cassino and at the Universities of Naples, Cologne, and Paris, earning a Master's degree. He never received Holy Orders and virtually his entire life was spent in teaching and writing.

His greatest work was the *Summa Theologica,* a masterful systematic statement of doctrine. It was by no means an immediate success, but time has proven it to be one of the finest intellectual expositions of the Christian faith ever composed. Some three centuries after his demise he was declared "Universal Teacher" to the church. He was particularly concerned about the relationship of faith and reason. He successfully reconciled the philosophy of Aristotle and Christian doctrine.

Thomas's intellectual genius was matched by a deep devotion to the Lord and by a rich spiritual and ethical life. He wrote many hymns, six of which appear in the *Hymnal 1940* (numbers 193, 194, 199, 200, 204, and 209).

O God, by whose Holy Spirit is given to one the word of wisdom, and to another the word of knowledge, and to another the word of faith: We praise your Name for the gifts of grace imparted to your servant Thomas, through whose teaching we know you better.

Presentation of our Lord Jesus Christ in the Temple

The Purification of Saint Mary the Virgin

Ancient Jewish custom prescribed that a woman who had borne a male child should, forty days after giving birth, come to the Temple to be "purified" (Leviticus 12). Furthermore, it was customary to publicly present every male child to God in the Temple (Exodus 13:2 and 12). Therefore, Mary and Joseph went up to the Temple for her Purification and Jesus' Presentation.

In the Temple, to everyone's surprise, a devout old man, Simeon, who was full of the Holy Spirit and "waiting for the consolation of Israel," took the infant Jesus in his arms and praised God in the words of the now familiar *Nunc dimittis*. In this canticle Simeon proclaimed Jesus "a light to lighten the Gentiles." For this reason, in medieval times the *Nunc dimittis* was sung and candles were blessed and lit and carried in procession through the streets on the night of this feast. It is still called "Candlemas" in England and the ancient "Feast of Lights" is still sometimes observed in connection with this occasion. Certainly a reflection on the *Nunc dimittis* (Prayer Book, page 28) is always an appropriate devotion for this day.

Almighty God, we pray that as your only Son our Savior was presented in the temple of the old covenant, so we, who are the temple of his Holy Spirit, may come before you with pure and clean hearts.

Anskar

Archbishop of Hamburg

Missionary to Denmark and Sweden

This Saxon monk of Corbie, France, was one of the first Christian missionaries to the notorious Vikings. Most of the descendants of the Vikings are today's Danes, Swedes, and Norwegians. However, a significant Viking strain entered England through the Danelaw and the Norman Conquest.

Anskar established the first Christian school in Denmark, but was soon run out by local heathens. Undiscouraged, he moved on to Sweden where he founded that country's first Christian church in about 832. His interest in the Vikings did not wane when he accepted a call as bishop of Hamburg in Germany. He continued to initiate missions, especially in Sweden. It was not until long after his death that Sweden became a Christian country, but he had sown the seeds of her conversion, and it is for this reason that he is highly honored in Sweden to this day.

The Church of England has enjoyed centuries of happy relations with the Scandinavian churches, especially with the Church of Sweden. The Episcopal Church in America includes "Old Swedes" churches which were established by the Church of Sweden in colonial times. The feast of Anskar provides an appropriate occasion to thank God for the gift of brotherhood among Swedish, English, and American Christians.

O Lord, bless Anskar and the Scandanavian peoples.

Cornelius the Centurion

First Gentile Christian

Our Lord, of course, was Jewish. Some felt that the Christ had come to the Jews alone and that one must first become a Jew in order to become a Christian.

Cornelius was a Gentile and a centurion (an officer in the Roman Army) stationed at Caesarea. He was widely respected among the Jews, not only because of his important position but also because he gave liberally to the poor and "honored God as they did." He was called "upright and God-fearing." He learned of Jesus Christ from the Apostle Peter, received the Holy Spirit and was baptised.

It was Cornelius' profession of faith that led Peter to exclaim, "God has shown me that I should not call any man common or unclean. . . . God shows no partiality, but in every nation anyone who fears him and does what is right is acceptable to him." Perhaps the testimony of Cornelius would be helpful to those in our own time who see Christianity as a purely cultural or racial thing. He is a fitting patron for the career soldier.

O God, who by your Spirit did call Cornelius the Centurion to be the first Christian among the Gentiles: Grant to your Church in every nation a ready mind and will to proclaim your love to all who turn to you with unfeigned hope and faith; for the sake of Jesus Christ our Lord, who lives and reigns with you and the same Spirit ever, one God, world without end.

The Martyrs of Japan

A Community that Kept the Faith

Japan was first introduced to Christianity by Francis Xavier, a great Roman Catholic missionary. For nearly half a century the churches he founded flourished and grew. Finally, the Japanese government became alarmed at the spread of Christianity which they regarded as a cloak for subversive activity by foreigners. Christianity was made illegal, and to show that the authorities meant business, twenty-six Japanese Christians were publicly crucified in Nagasaki.

But this was only the beginning. For the next two hundred and fifty years, if a Japanese were found to be practicing Christianity he was subject to the death penalty. Through the years many thousands died rather than forsake Christ. At last the ban was lifted in 1859. Christian missionaries again entered Japan (see Channing Moore Williams, December 2). To their astonishment they discovered several secret Christian communities still surviving, without priests and with very little education, but still keeping the Faith in a most admirable manner, as they had through centuries of persecution.

Almighty God, by whose grace and power your holy martyrs in Japan triumphed over suffering, and were faithful even to death: Grant us, who now remember them in thanksgiving, to be so faithful in our witness to you in this world, that we may receive with them the crown of everlasting life.

21

Cyril (Monk) and Methodius (Bishop)

February 14, 869 and 885

Missionaries to the Slavs

Apostles and Scholars

These brothers, Cyril and Methodius, were chiefly responsible for the conversion of the Slavic people of Eastern Europe in the ninth century. They were from Thessalonica, Greece. Each was educated at the great university at Constantinople, and each initially took up a career there; Cyril, the younger, as professor of philosophy and Methodius, the elder, as a librarian. Cyril was the first to do missionary work. He worked among the Tartars of what is now the Soviet Ukraine.

The brothers went together as missionaries to Moravia (part of modern Czechoslovakia). Cyril invented an alphabet for the Slavic tongues of that area. Together they translated the Liturgy and the Scriptures into Slavonic, the language of the people.

The task of converting these Slavs was not easy and was made even more difficult by the competitive spirit of the various Christian groups nearby. There was pressure from the Roman Church to impose the Latin language on the population and pressure from Germanic Christians to accept the Arian heresy. However, Cyril and Methodius did not allow partisan strife to interfere with their evangelistic work, and they eventually gained the admiration of all parties. Methodius was consecrated Archbishop of Sirmium in 869, with the blessing of both Rome and Orthodoxy. Cyril died in that same year.

Thomas Bray

Priest and Missionary

Died February 15, 1730

Humanitarian and Educator

The church in colonial America was often neglected and badly used by both Englishmen and Americans. But she found a great champion in Thomas Bray, the Bishop of London's "Commissary" to Maryland. Bray was an Oxford professor as well as a priest. He took very seriously the task of educating poor clergymen, laymen, and children. His understanding and concern for America's Indians and Negroes was far ahead of his time. He founded church libraries and schools in England and America, raised money for missionary endeavors, and influenced young English priests to try their vocations in America.

Bray fought long and hard to get an American bishop consecrated, but failed. He founded two of our church's most effective missionary organizations, the SPCK and the SPG (now USPG), both of which are still in operation after two and a half centuries of work the world over.

The deplorable condition of England's prisons was of grave concern to Thomas Bray. He organized Sunday "Beef and Beer" dinners in those prisons and went to Parliament with proposals for prison reform. It was Thomas Bray who first suggested to General Oglethorpe the idea of founding a humanitarian colony for the relief of honest debtors, but he died before seeing this, the Georgia colony, a reality. Few clergymen have taken more seriously our Lord's command, "Feed my sheep."

Polycarp

Bishop and Martyr of Smyrna

A Man of Courage

Polycarp, Bishop of Smyrna in what is now called Turkey, did not seek martyrdom and did not encourage others to do so. When persecution broke out Polycarp made every honorable effort to protect his flock and himself. He even hid in the country but, eventually, the authorities found him.

Since Christians worshipped Jesus Christ, an "unauthorized god," and since they refused to worship the Roman gods or the "Divine Caesar," they were considered atheists and subversives. At a great public festival in the arena in Smyrna, Polycarp was presented to the governor amid cries of "Kill the atheist!" from the excited and unruly mob. The governor admonished Polycarp to swear by Caesar and to revile Christ and thereby save himself. The old bishop's famous reply was, "For eighty-six years I have been his servant and he has done me no wrong; how can I blaspheme my King who has saved me? . . . You pretend not to know who I am, let me tell you plainly, I am a Christian. If you want to learn the doctrine of Christianity, set a day and hear me." Polycarp was publicly burned to death.

The Christians in Smyrna who escaped death in this wave of persecution wrote a letter describing the execution of their great bishop and sent it to other churches. We still have this famous letter, "The Martyrdom of Polycarp."

24

Matthias

Apostle

Judas' betrayal of Jesus and his subsequent suicide left a vacancy in the fellowship of the Apostles. The remaining eleven Apostles resolved to fill that vacancy and in so doing set an important precedent for the church.

The first chapter of the Acts of the Apostles tells us that two men were nominated, Joseph Barsabas and Matthias. The Apostles prayed for the guidance of the Holy Spirit and then cast lots to see which of the two should be chosen. The lot fell to Matthias who was then enrolled with the Apostles. The Apostles were, therefore, deemed fit, under the guidance of the Holy Spirit, to select and appoint new Apostles as some died or fell away. It was partly on this precedent that the Apostolic Succession was based. It is interesting to note that even today in America a bishop's election must be with the consent of the House of Bishops and is not considered proper until the new bishop is consecrated by several bishops.

We know nothing of Matthias' life following the events described in Acts. Tradition holds that he was an exemplary bishop and on his feast day we pray that the church might always be "ordered and guided by faithful and true pastors."

Almighty God, who chose your faithful servant Matthias to be counted among the twelve: Grant that your Church may be ordered and guided by faithful and true pastors.

George Herbert

Died February 27, 1633

Priest

Poet and Pastor

George Herbert was brilliant, wealthy, well-born, hand-some, and a favorite of the King and Court. To the astonishment of a generation of prominent Englishmen, he abandoned a promising career in public life, took Holy Orders, and accepted a call to the humble parishes of Fugglestone and Bemerton. As he put it, "Methought I heard one calling, 'Child.' And I replied, 'My Lord.' "

In his short life (George Herbert was only forty when he died) he made a lasting contribution to the church's life. He wrote *A Priest to the Temple; or the Country Parson.* He wrote many excellent poems and hymns (see *The Hymnal 1940,* numbers 290 and 476). Most important of all, he left us a beautiful example of a small town pastor. It was in tiny Bemerton, and not at the mighty Court of St. James, that George Herbert found depth and meaning in life. At Bemerton he was able to witness for his Master in unselfish service to others. He had learned an age old lesson. "Nothing," he wrote, "is little in God's service."

O eternal Lord God, who holds all souls in life: We beseech you to shed forth upon your whole Church in paradise and on earth the bright beams of your light and thy peace; and grant that we, following the good examples of your servant George Herbert, and of all those who loved and served you here, may at the last enter with them into your unending joy.

David

Bishop of Menevia

Apostle to Wales

When the Roman legions were withdrawn in the fifth century a nightmare of chaos and terror closed in on isolated Britain. England fell into the hands of the heathen Angles, Saxons, and Jutes and it appeared that Christianity might disappear from the Islands altogether. Some Celtic Christians withdrew into Wales and David emerged as their most effective leader.

David was a monk of noble birth, well educated, and a famous teacher and preacher. We have little concrete historical data concerning him. Even his name (probably Dawi) seems to have been distorted with the passage of time. We do know that he founded several monastic communities in Wales, and that these served as places of refuge for the homeless, as centers for the spread of Christianity, and as bastions of learning, justice, and good order in a hostile environment. David was the abbot-bishop of the monastery at Menevia. He, and other hearty pioneer monks like him, kept the light of the gospel shining in a very dark and troubled time.

O Almighty God, who did choose your servant David to be an apostle to the people of Wales, to bring those who were wandering in darkness and error to the true light and knowledge of you: Grant us to walk in that same light.

27

Chad

Bishop of Lichfield

A Leader who Learned to Change

In the seventh century sweeping changes were being made in church administration and in the forms of worship to which British people were accustomed. Chad, who had been educated at the great Celtic monastery at Lindisfarne, was a spokesman for the opposition to these changes. At the Synod of Whitby he defended the Celtic forms of worship and Celtic church order. But the Synod decided in favor of the Roman ways of doing things. Chad gracefully accepted the decision of the Synod and helped enforce the observation of the new liturgy.

Later Chad was appointed Bishop of York by the King, following the custom of the day. Meanwhile, Wilfred had been made Bishop of York by the Archbishop of Canterbury and the Roman Pope. Chad accepted the church's new way of doing things and resigned in favor of Wilfred. The Archbishop of Canterbury was so thankful and so impressed with Chad's humility and devotion to duty that he made him Bishop of Lichfield. There Chad lived very simply, not even affording himself the luxury of a horse, and exerted a powerful influence for holiness and sound religious practice.

Grant to us, your humble servants, a like faith and power of love you enkindled as a flame in the heart of your servant Chad.

John and
Charles Wesley

Priests

March 3, Died 1791, 1788

Eighteenth Century Evangelicals

John and Charles were raised together at the rectory in Epworth. They studied together at Oxford and together they were ordained into the ministry of the Church of England. Together they journeyed to America and served together as missionaries in Georgia for the Society for the Propagation of the Gospel. Together they led the great evangelical revival of the eighteenth century.

This movement attempted to foster among Christians a strong personal commitment to Jesus. Its leaders, such as John and Charles, preached and sang in the open fields, on street corners, and in the market places. They actively opposed slavery and drunkenness. John was the more impressive preacher, Charles the musician. (*The Hymnal 1940* contains eighteen of Charles' hymns.)

The Evangelical Movement led to the formation of several religious societies. The most famous of these was the "Methodist" Society, so-called for its strict and methodical practices. Some of these societies, especially in America, separated from the English Church. John and Charles Wesley, however, did not forsake the Church of England. Their feast day would seem an appropriate time to recommit ourselves to the spread of Christ's Kingdom among all classes of men.

Perpetua and her Companions

Martyrs of Carthage

The wealthy widow Perpetua, of Carthage, not only became a Christian but she opened her home to Christian worship. When this was discovered by the authorities, she and several of her friends were imprisoned. Perpetua's small child was cruelly taken from her. One of her prison companions, Felicitas, a slave girl, gave birth to a baby while in prison. The baby was taken from her, also, as in the case of Perpetua. However, to the great relief of all the incarcerated companions, the baby was secretly adopted by Christian parents.

The experiences of the companions in prison, including the dreams and visions of Perpetua, were recorded and remain one of our most valuable documents of early Christianity. The companions were sentenced to be thrown to wild beasts in the arena. Their last act together was to exchange the kiss of peace. They went joyfully and triumphantly to their fate, Perpetua calmly tidying her veil in the face of the hideous onslaught.

Almighty and everlasting God, with whom your meek ones go forth as the mighty: Grant us so to cherish the memory of thy blessed martyrs Perpetua and her companions, that we may share their pure and steadfast faith in you; through Jesus Christ our Lord.

Gregory

Bishop of Nyssa

Teacher of Christian Doctrine

At a time such as ours, when some persons take the spurious art of astrology so seriously, a Christian might well read this ancient Christian teacher's book on the subject, entitled *Against Fate*. This was one of many writings by Gregory against various forms of wrong thinking and wretched living.

Gregory was a brother of Basil the Great (see June 14) and served for many years as the Bishop of Nyssa in Cappadocia, a part of central Turkey today. He was a powerful preacher, a brilliant student of the Bible, and a deeply spiritual person. We still have a number of his sermons, biblical commentaries, and devotional and ascetical writings. Gregory attended the great Church Council at Constantinople in 381 and staunchly opposed the Arians. The Arians wrongly regarded Jesus Christ as only an agent of God rather than as the God-Man. Because of his convincing argumentation at this Council, Gregory came to be called the "Pillar of Orthodoxy." Through the years, his wise counsels and sound teachings led many into a fuller understanding of the Faith and saved many others from much unhappiness and error.

Enlighten by your Holy Spirit those who teach and those who learn, that, rejoicing in the knowledge of your truth, they may worship and serve you.

Gregory the Great
Bishop of Rome

Died March 12, 604

Renowned for Music

At a time when it looked as though England would be lost to heathenism forever, Gregory, Bishop of Rome, observed some handsome Anglo-Saxon lads being sold in the slave market and, moved with compassion, resolved to dispatch missionaries to England (see May 26). Within fifty years England was calling herself a Christian country and, furthermore, the Celtic Christians of the British Isles had been integrated into the Roman Church.

Gregory was no ordinary bishop! He was a patrician, a senator's son, and he had served as "mayor" of the city for some time before he decided to enter a monastery. Even after becoming a monk he served in a semi-governmental position as representative of the Bishop of Rome in the Imperial Capital, Constantinople.

It was in the year 590 that Gregory was elected bishop. He proved to be one of the most talented and effective bishops of history and, fortunately, he left us an excellent book on the subject, entitled *Pastoral Care*. He coined the title "Servant of the Servants of God" for his office. With virtually no help from the Imperial government he gained a lasting peace in war-torn Italy, and he organized the church in Western Europe to withstand the assaults of the Germanic and Viking invasions. He encouraged and contributed to a form of music which still bears his name, Gregorian Chant.

Patrick

Bishop and Missionary

Apostle to Ireland

Scarcely any saint has been as celebrated as Patrick. Few have been more deserving. He was born of Christian parents in Roman Britain. At sixteen he was captured by barbarian raiders and carried off to Ireland as a slave. After six years as a swineherd he escaped and eventually returned to Britain. To the astonishment of family and friends, he resolved to return to Ireland as a missionary, and he began a long period of intensive training in France. After many hardships and disappointments he was able to return to the land of his bondage as a missionary bishop.

Patrick was not the first Christian missionary to Ireland but he was by far the most successful. Patrick himself has left us a record of his experiences in his *Confessions*—how he confronted the fierce King at Tara and how he confounded the proud Druids. His sound and effective teaching is reflected in a hymn, "I bind unto myself today" (see *The Hymnal 1940,* number 268).

Most of Patrick's work was done in the northern part of the island. His headquarters were at Armagh. He made a famous pilgrimage into the mountains of Mayo. He died at Saul in Ulster. It is said that he found a heathen Ireland but left a Christian one.

Bless your servant Patrick, O Lord, and all the people of Ireland.

Cyril

Bishop of Jerusalem

Great Teacher and Pastor

When famine hit the vicinity of Jerusalem, Cyril, the bishop, promptly sold some of the church's most prized possessions to relieve the poor and to obtain food for the starving. When the famine was over some angry church members succeeded in having Cyril condemned at a public meeting as an irresponsible thief who had illegally disposed of church property. They temporarily drove him out of the city. Although Cyril was a gentle and conciliatory man, this event was typical of the bitter controversy which racked his episcopate.

Scarcely had he regained his diocese before he was again expelled. This time by Arian heretics who had gained great power in Jerusalem. He was restored to the Jerusalem bishophric again by none other than the infamous Emperor Julian, the Apostate. Due to this rather coincidental fact, Cyril had difficulty regaining the confidence of the other orthodox bishops of the church. Furthermore, the Jerusalem Church had become notorious throughout the Christian world for its low moral standards. This situation Cyril attempted to correct, but his enemies blamed him for it.

Cyril's greatest talent seems to have been as a teacher and preacher. Very little of his thought was ever written down, but what we have is most impressive and timely even today.

Joseph

Foster-father of Jesus

In the face of circumstance that might have distressed a man of less stature, Joseph graciously assumed the role of Jesus' father. He is well remembered in Christian tradition for the love he showed to the boy Jesus who lived "under his roof" for at least twelve years. Joseph's tender affection and care for Mary has, likewise, been long celebrated in the church.

Joseph was a pious Jew, a descendant of David. He was a carpenter by trade, a man of very modest means, with no education outside the synagogue. It is generally believed that he died quietly and naturally, prior to our Lord's active ministry. The gospel writers tell us that Jesus was widely known as the "son of Joseph the carpenter," and Joseph's influence on him was, of course, inestimable. Jesus could not have had anyone less in mind than Joseph when he called God "father." Yet Joseph could not have had more than a vague inkling of the importance of his humble life. His life is a testimony to the value of simple everyday human things, especially that human thing called "fatherhood."

O God, who did call blessed Joseph to be the faithful guardian of your only-begotten Son, and the spouse of his virgin Mother: Give us grace to follow his example in constant worship of you and obedience to your commands, that our homes may be sanctified by your presence, and our children nurtured in your fear and love; through the same Jesus Christ our Lord.

Cuthbert

Bishop of Lindisfarne

Apostle to Northumbria

A man of large stature and unusual physical prowess, Cuthbert seemed destined from his youth for leadership. He, however, was always concerned that his spiritual leadership match his physical endowments. Prior to accepting a call to become Bishop of Lindisfarne, he spent eight years in prayer and meditation on the cold and isolated island of Farne.

Cuthbert's episcopate was brief but highly significant. It was occasioned by plague, war, and schism. He spent much time caring for and healing the sick and preaching against the superstitious use of charms and amulets. In the midst of war Bishop Cuthbert went fearlessly among his people, ministering to the wounded and inspiring hope in the survivors. He worked toward the reconciliation of those Celtic Christians who were dissatisfied with the liturgical and political changes being effected by the Roman Church in Britain.

Cuthbert led many men to salvation in Christ and contributed significantly to the Christianization of the North Country of England. Yet, holy living to Cuthbert meant a life of service. As the historian Bede put it, "He was aflame with the fire of divine charity; and to give counsel and help to the weak he considered equal to an act of prayer—knowing that he who said, 'Thou shalt love the Lord thy God' also said, 'Thou shalt love thy neighbor.' "

Thomas Ken

Died March 21, 1711

Bishop of Bath and Wells

A Symbol of Constancy

Most Americans are familiar with the Doxology, "Praise God from whom all blessings flow" (*The Hymnal 1940*, number 139), but few will recognize the name of its author, Thomas Ken. He was one of those rare souls who steered a straight course through the troubled waters of seventeenth century England.

Defending the "Via Media," he boldly defied three kings: James II, whose edicts Ken refused to read in church; Charles II, whose marital infidelity he condemned; and William of Orange, whose legal right to the throne he denied. This last protestation cost Ken his diocese. After more than ten years of wandering about jobless and homeless, he was finally reconciled to the Church of England under Queen Anne. He was then too old and infirm to resume the work of a bishop.

Thomas Ken was a masterful teacher, hymn writer, and pastor. He always lived very simply and he never married. The words of his will are a classic statement of his faith. "I die in the Holy, Catholic, and Apostolic Faith, professed by the whole Church, before the disunion of East and West: more particularly I die in the communion of the Church of England, as it stands distinguished from all Papal and Puritan Innovations."

O God, we give you thanks for the purity and strength with which you did endow your servant Thomas Ken.

James De Koven

Priest

Defender of Our Catholic Heritage

Success in the world's terms is not a usual reward for great and good men. James De Koven was certainly one of the greatest and best leaders of the Episcopal Church in the nineteenth century, yet his advice was rarely heeded. He was never made a bishop. The college he so carefully fathered no longer exists.

He was closely associated with the unpopular Ritualist party in a time when the church's life was especially marred by partisan strife. He succeeded in getting the General Convention to accept the fact that the viewpoints of the ritualists were at least not subversive. Through his reasoned and compelling oratory in defense of the catholic heritage, he enabled the church to stand above the petty sectarianism of the day and reaffirm its comprehensive nature. Perhaps his greatest achievement was in preventing the Episcopal Church from adopting a rigid, doctrinaire, and exclusive confession, after the manner of Protestantism.

James De Koven was a scholar and one of the really fine Christian educators of his day. He was a graduate of Columbia and of the General Theological Seminary in New York. He was a professor at Nashotah House and Warden of Racine College in Wisconsin for twenty years. He was an excellent pastor and a man "continuous in prayer."

Gregory the Illuminator

Died March 23, c.332

Bishop and Missionary

Apostle to Armenia

The first Christian kingdom in history was Armenia, now a part of the Soviet Union. Armenia was converted through the efforts of Gregory. This kingdom came to an unhappy end as an independent state in A.D. 430, yet some two and one-half million persons today are still culturally Armenians. They enjoy a racial, linguistic, and religious heritage which is one of the world's oldest and richest. Their community has endured fifteen-hundred years of dispersion, harassment, and often severe persecution.

The truly marvelous story of Christian Armenia began when the infant Gregory, who was a prince by birth, was exiled by enemies and reared by a compassionate Christian family in Cappadocia (modern central Turkey). As an adult and a Christian he returned to Armenia and converted the King, Tiridates, heir of Gregory's old enemies. This was not done easily. Indeed, many legends have grown up around the tradition of Gregory's great difficulties, hardships, and sufferings in effecting the conversion of the king and subsequently the kingdom. For this work he is called the "illuminator." Gregory was eventually consecrated Bishop of Etchmiadzin and was the organizer of the Armenian Church.

The Episcopal Church has enjoyed a warm and friendly relationship with the Armenian Church for many years. Offer thanks for that friendship.

The Annunciation of our Lord Jesus Christ to the Blessed Virgin Mary

The Lord's Birth Foretold

Not only one of the most important, but also one of the most touching events described in the gospel, is Luke's account of the visit of the angel Gabriel to Mary and of Mary's response. The angel's salutation, "Hail, O favoured one, the Lord is with you!" was certainly startling. The angel's announcement must have been frightening and deeply perplexing. "You will conceive and bear a son . . . , and he will be great and will be called the Son of the Most High . . . , and will reign over the house of Jacob forever; and of his kingdom there will be no end." It is not difficult to imagine trembling in her voice when Mary asked, "How can this be?"

When the angel had finished his explanation, Mary freely agreed to submit to God's will in the matter, saying, "Behold the handmaid of the Lord. May it be with me as you have said." So we, who are the church in this age, are called upon to respond obediently and confidently to God's will for us. One is reminded of Isaiah's response when he was called upon to do the Lord's work in his generation, "Here am I, send me." It is also interesting and comforting to note that neither Mary nor Isaiah was forced into submission, but rather, "in the fullness of time" each responded willingly, gracefully, and positively, having little idea of what lay ahead.

40

John Keble

Died March 20, 1866

Priest

Shepherd of the Oxford Movement

On July 14, 1833, before a distinguished group of judges assembled in the Church of St. Mary the Virgin, Oxford, John Keble preached a startling sermon entitled "National Apostasy." He accused the English government of forsaking its ancient and sacred commitment to Christ and his church. This sermon marked the beginning of the "Oxford" or "Tractarian" Movement which shook the English church and nation to its roots.

The movement aimed at rescuing the institutional church from rampant "liberalizing" reforms which threatened to render the church impotent. Renewed emphasis was placed on the idea of the church as a divine institution, on the historic episcopate, and on the Book of Common Prayer.

Of the many eminent churchmen who took part in this movement, John Keble was perhaps the most mature and certainly one of the best loved. His unquestioned loyalty to the Church of England, his wise and gentle leadership, held the movement together and prevented many defections from Christianity on the one hand and to the Roman Church on the other. In the face of bitter controversy, there was no guile found in him.

His religious poetry had such a fresh, simple, and straight-forward quality about it that it remains popular today (see *The Hymnal 1940,* numbers 155, 166).

Thomas Cranmer

Archbishop of Canterbury

English Reformer

As Archbishop of Canterbury during the reigns of both Henry VIII and Edward VI, Cranmer presided over the reform of the Church of England. He was the chief composer of the *Book of Common Prayer* and contributed significantly to the translation of the *Bible* into English. He was one of the foremost scholars of his day, an eminent student of the Holy Scripture and the Liturgy.

Cranmer was convinced that a thorough reform of the church was needed in his day. He was a staunch opponent of the Papacy and one of those who declared the "Bishop of Rome hath no more authority in England than any other foreign bishop." However, he accepted episcopal orders and he did not favour the total dissolution of the monasteries.

When Mary Tudor, called "Bloody Mary" in English folklore, ascended the throne, Cranmer was imprisoned and convicted of heresy. For this he was burned at the stake at Oxford on March 21, 1556. Prior to the execution he had, under duress, signed recantations repudiating his reforming activities. For this he publicly repented and at the stake he is said to have willfully placed his right hand into the flames, saying, "This hand hath offended." His dying day was the noblest of his life.

Praise God for Cranmer and all martyrs and reformers in all ages.

John Donne

Priest

Died March 31, 1631

Poet and Preacher

"No man is an island. . . ." These oft-quoted words
from John Donne are not only a terse statement of a
universal truth, they point to a perplexing dilemma in
this great man's life. How could John Donne be reconciled to the baffling world in which he lived; an age
struggling with change, shattered by "the new learning,"
"the new art," "the new science," "the new government," and even "the new religion"? He felt deeply his
own responsibility to deal with these changes. He refused to retreat to an "island."

Donne went through a troubled and reckless youth,
characterized by cavalier gaiety on the one hand and
by deep-seated anxiety on the other. His elegant poetry
and the brilliance of his personality gained him many
influential friends, but little success otherwise. He married, but could hardly be said to have "settled down."
His charming wife bore him lovely children, but peace
and satisfaction did not enter his life until he took his
life to the Master.

Finally, he plunged himself into the church's life with
all the fervour of his cavalier days. He was ordained
and, after serving as a royal chaplain and as rector of
Sevenoaks, he became Dean of St. Paul's, London.
There he preached many celebrated sermons. His hearers
were astonished and many of their lives were profoundly
changed. His works have continued to stimulate thinkers
and writers into our own time.

Frederick Denison Maurice   *Died April 1, 1812*
Priest

Theologian and Social Reformer

In 1848 virtually all of Europe was aflame with revolution. Governments were violently overthrown in France, Germany, and Austria. The Establishment in England shuddered and reacted rather fearfully. At least one Christian theologian, F. D. Maurice, responded positively and set to work to apply Christian principles in the acute area of social reform.

Maurice, along with John Ludlow and Charles Kingsley, organized the Christian Socialists. They publicized the use of Christian attitudes in solving social problems. They helped organize trade unions and promoted reform legislation. Their ideas and actions were unpopular with certain persons of the Establishment and Maurice was forced to resign his post in theology at King's College.

Undeterred, Maurice founded a Workingmen's College in London and pioneered in the field of education for working class people. He wrote and published many volumes, the most famous of which was entitled *The Kingdom of Christ*.

Maurice laid the groundwork for much modern English theology. He forged contacts between the church and the reforming movements in the state and thereby helped prevent in England the antagonism which typyfied church-state relations in some countries as these reforming groups began to take the reins of government.

James Lloyd Breck

Died April 2, 1876

Priest

Pioneer Missionary and Educator

James Breck was a pioneer in several ways. He was a pioneer in the revival of monasticism in our church. He was a pioneer missionary to the Old Northwest and to California. He was a pioneer in theological education, being instrumental in the founding of both Nashotah House and Seabury theological seminaries.

Breck was a native of Philadelphia and a graduate of the University of Pennsylvania and the General Seminary in New York. He joined two classmates in forming an experimental religious community under the direction of Bishop Kemper (see May 24) in the great wilderness of Wisconsin. There he lived in utmost simplicity and spent virtually every waking hour in religious work.

Indefatigable, Breck founded numerous churches, missions, and schools. He prayed, taught, traveled, and worked tirelessly to initiate and keep going the work of the church. Himself an ardent Anglo-Catholic, Breck rejoiced in the renewed emphasis on catholic doctrine and worship in his day. He preached and exemplified the extension of Christian discipline into every aspect of living.

In later years, with the church firmly established in Wisconsin and Minnesota, James Breck sought sunnier climes. He went to California and vanished into legend, a veritable "Johnny Appleseed" of the church.

Thank you for your servant James, indefatigable founder.

Richard

Bishop of Chichester

A Most Compassionate Scholar

Richard of Chichester was a tireless student of theology, a man constant in devotion to the Lord, and one whose life was filled with unselfish service to his fellowmen.

Although he was born to a prosperous family, Richard was orphaned at an early age and soon impoverished by a negligent guardian. He entered Oxford unable to afford even a gown or a fire in winter. Yet he did very well in his studies and was eventually able to go on to further study at the University of Paris and at Bologna.

He returned to England as a small-town parson, a role he always loved. However, his fame as a counselor and preacher soon spread far and wide. Against the wishes of King Henry III, Richard was consecrated Bishop of Chichester. The king denied him access to the cathedral and to the bishop's palace, so Richard spent two years wandering barefoot through his diocese, living very simply on the charity of his flock.

When the quarrel with the king was finally settled and Richard moved into the palace, he lived there almost as a beggar, wearing a hair shirt, fasting often, and sleeping on the floor. He was an efficient administrator and a stern disciplinarian when the occasion called for it. Yet he entertained the poor lavishly and ultimately willed his episcopal estate to the poor, to hospitals, to widows and orphans.

See hymn 429, *The Hymnal 1940,* by Richard of Chichester.

William Augustus Muhlenberg

Died April 8, 1877

Priest

Pastor and Humanitarian

The personality and character of this man captured the imagination of the entire Episcopal Church in the nineteenth century. He was claimed by all parties, calling himself an "Evangelical Catholic." He was an enthusiastic exponent of Maurice's ideas of Christian social involvement (see April 1). He was remarkably versatile, an excellent preacher, schoolmaster, and poet (see *The Hymnal 1940*, number 15).

For over forty years he served parishes in Pennsylvania and New York and became one of the most widely loved and trusted pastors of his day. Some consider the founding of St. Lukes Hospital in New York City his greatest achievement. However, he also founded two religious communities and a number of schools and contributed to the organization of several public charities.

Muhlenberg long exercised an important influence in the General Convention and the activities of the National Church. He was the chief author of the "Muhlenberg Memorial," a document which profoundly affected the life of the Episcopal Church. He was instrumental in initiating significant Prayer Book and Hymnal revision. In proposing his name for the Church's Calendar the Standing Liturgical Commission declared, "There was not a significant area of the church's life that he did not elevate and strengthen."

William Law

Died April 9, 1761

Priest

Renowned Pastor and Author

"If we are to follow Christ, it must be in our common way of spending every day." So wrote William Law in *A Serious Call to the Devout and Holy Life.* This quiet schoolmaster of Putney, England, could hardly be considered a revolutionary, yet his book had near revolutionary repercussions. His challenge to take Christian living very seriously received more enthusiastic response than he could have imagined, especially in the lives of William Carey, Henry Venn, George Whitefield, and the Wesley brothers, all of whom he strongly influenced. More than any other man, William Law lay the foundation for the religious revival of the eighteenth century, the Evangelical Movement in England, and the Great Awakening in America.

William Law came to typify the devout parson in the eyes of many. His life was characterized by simplicity, devotion, and the pursuits of charity. Because he was a Non-Juror he was deprived of the usual means of making a living as a clergyman in the Church of England. He therefore worked as a tutor (in the famous Gibbon household) and as a sort of "free-lance" minister. He organized schools and homes for poor children. He stoutly defended the sacraments and the scriptures against the flagrant attacks of the Deists. He spoke out eloquently against the ghastly warfare of his day. His richly inspired sermons and writings have gained him a permanent place in Christian literature.

George Augustus Selwyn   *Died April 12, 1878*

Bishop

Missionary to New Zealand and Melanesia

The first Bishop of New Zealand was trained at Eton and Cambridge and had credentials, talent, and influence enough to have lived a most comfortable and successful life in England. Instead, he chose to go half way around the world and live for nearly two decades under the most trying circumstances, forging the foundations of a new branch of the church in a most troubled land. It is exhausting even to read of his journeys through the islands of Melanesia and New Zealand, using the unsophisticated and sometimes hazardous nineteenth century modes of transport in an often hostile land.

Bishop Selwyn was a tireless evangelist, pastor, teacher, organizer, and administrator. Perhaps most important of all he gained the respect, indeed the love, of the native Maoris to whom he first brought the light of the gospel. During a decade of cruel and tragic warfare between the English colonists and the Maoris, he was able to bring the ministrations of Christ to both sides. Finally, he was able to play a reconciling role in the establishment of peace.

He was elected Bishop of Lichfield, England, in 1868 and held that office for the last ten years of his life. He was a capable scholar and a man of many interests, exercising influence in both the church and state.

We thank you for your servant George and his ministry in New Zealand.

49

Alphege

Archbishop of Canterbury

Martyr and Witness to the Danes

"From the wrath of the Northmen, Good Lord, deliver us." So prayed the English monks, but their prayer seemed of no avail. In 1011 Canterbury itself was besieged and taken by the fierce Danish Vikings. They carried the Archbishop, Alphege, off in their ships and demanded a ransom.

Alphege was an old and kindly monk from Deerhurst and later Abbot of Bath. He had been elected Bishop of Winchester under Dunstan (see May 19). For five years he had served as one of the most beloved and effective Archbishops ever to hold the See of Canterbury. He played a part in the conversion of King Olaf of Norway. Now Alphege was harshly bound, half-starved, and shamefully abused.

Englishmen immediately began raising the ransom, but Alphege, knowing how impoverished his people were already, refused to permit it. The enraged Vikings, in a drunken frenzy, fell upon the old Archbishop and savagely beat him to death. Yet, a number of them had been so impressed with the faith and compassion of their prisoner that they soon presented themselves for baptism.

Grant us, in like manner to your servant Alphege, constancy in faith and truth, and to fear none of the world's adversaries.

Anselm

Died April 21, 1109

Archbishop of Canterbury

Doctor of the Church

Anselm lived in an age when ignorance and raw power often went hand in hand. His life was spent in opposing these enslaving forces, especially in England.

He was born of noble Christian parents in Burgundy and educated at the monasteries at St. Leger and Bec in Normandy. He joined the latter community and, after an impressive career as teacher and author, became its abbot. He first visited England at the invitation of William the Conqueror, by whom he was well loved. His consecration as Archbishop of Canterbury met with overwhelming approval from the English people, who knew him as a wise and compassionate person.

He spent years in this high office attempting to gain a lasting peace in a time of constant feuding. He championed the church's independence from royal authority and was twice exiled by angry kings whose bidding he refused to do.

Anselm was a theologian of the first order. He lectured in Rome, carried on intellectual correspondence with the most brilliant leaders of his day, and wrote a number of books that are still highly regarded among theologians. His most famous book, *Cur Deus Homo?* was the foremost work on the doctrine of the atonement to come out of the Middle Ages.

O God, continue to enlighten us by the teaching of your servant Anselm.

Mark

Evangelist

Tradition holds that Mark (sometimes John Mark) was the boy who lost his clothes when Jesus was taken in the Garden of Gethsemene (see Mark 14:51). It is also thought by many that the "upper room" where the Last Supper was held was in Mark's parents' home. Mark's mother, whose name was Mary, was a follower of Jesus and a friend of the disciples.

The Apostle Peter seems to have taken young Mark "under his wing." Mark is listed by Paul as one of Peter's followers in the early controversies in the Jerusalem Church. Mark was also a missionary companion to Paul and a life-long friend of Barnabas. He was in Rome with Peter and Paul but escaped the Neronian persecution. According to the historian Eusebius, he traveled to Egypt and founded the great Alexandrian Church there. Also, it is believed that he was martyred there by a mob of angry pagans.

Mark is generally regarded as the author of the second gospel, which bears his name. It is sometimes called the "Gentile Gospel" because it seems to be directed more towards a Gentile than a Jewish audience.

Almighty God, we thank you for the gospel of your Son Jesus Christ, committed to his Church by the hand of your evangelist Saint Mark; and we pray that, being firmly grounded in its truth, we may be faithful to its teaching both in word and deed; through Jesus Christ our Lord.

Catherine of Sienna

Mystic and Humanitarian

One tends to think of medieval women as silent and passive dwellers in homes and convents. This was far from the case with Catherine of Sienna. She exercised great influence in matters of church and state and her's was one of the keenest minds of her day.

Her father was a merchant in the flourishing Italian town of Sienna. In her youth she had some extraordinary religious experiences which caused concern among her family and friends. At sixteen she joined the Third Order of St. Dominic and gave herself entirely to contemplation and the service of the sick and poor. Her reputation as a counselor and mystic soon spread far and wide. In 1376 she made a journey to Avignon and boldly confronted Pope Gregory XI who heeded her advice and thus averted schism and bloodshed.

Catherine's famous book, the *Dialogue,* is most unusual and highly symbolic. We have four hundred letters written by her, addressed to bishops, kings, scholars, merchants, and obscure peasants. They are excellent literature and reflect a wide range of interests.

Catherine spent countless months caring for the victims of plague. Again and again she was to be found in the courts of state, interceding for justice, mercy, and peace.

Deliver us, we pray, from an inordinate love of this world, that, following the example of your servant Catherine, we may serve you with singleness of heart.

Philip and James

Apostles

The Apostle Philip was from Bethsaida and was one of the Twelve. He is mentioned in all four gospels and figures prominently in two episodes in the Lord's ministry. In the first, the Feeding of the Five Thousand, his very practical nature shows through (see John 6:4f). The other episode is the gospel lesson for this feast (see John 14:6-13). He should not be confused with Philip, Deacon and Evangelist, who is mentioned in the fifth and eighth chapters of Acts.

James the Less, son of Alphaeus, was one of the Twelve also. He should not be confused with either James the son of Zebedee (see July 25) or James, the Lord's brother (see October 23). His agnomen "the less" may imply a small stature or youthfulness. He is only mentioned four times in Holy Scripture, and then briefly or in a list, so we know very little about him.

Philip and James are little more than names to us today. One cannot imagine their being saddened by this fact since this community and the Christ it knows lives on. "For what we preach is not ourselves, but Jesus Christ as Lord, with ourselves as your servants for Jesus' sake."

Almighty God, who gave to your apostles Saint Philip and Saint James grace and strength fearlessly to bear testimony to the truth: Grant that we, being always mindful of their victory of faith, may learn like them to overcome the world, and glorify the Name of our Lord Jesus Christ.

Athanasius

Died May 2, 373

Bishop of Alexandria

Most Orthodox Theologian

"Athanasius Contra Mundum"—Athanasius against the world. In this phrase Christians have for centuries summed up the great life and work of this wise Bishop of Alexandria, Egypt. Long ago he became a symbol of orthodoxy, of right and clear thinking in the face of overwhelming opposition.

His thinking was ahead of his time. As Christians came to know and understand his teaching they came to feel that he offered the most accurate intellectual expression of their faith. The doctrine he espoused eventually became the universal teaching of the church and embodied in the creeds, especially the one that bears his name, the Athanasian Creed.

This did not come easily. For a time it seemed that, indeed, the whole world was against Athanasius. His chief opponents, the Arians, gained control of the church. He was deposed and exiled and vilified. He died without seeing the victory of his position proclaimed at the General Council at Constantinople in 381.

Basically, he opposed the Arian teaching that Jesus Christ was less than God but more than man. He held that such a being would be of no benefit to either God or man and could not reconcile God and man. Athanasius taught that Jesus Christ was truly God and truly man. In his renowned treatise, *De Incarnatione,* he wrote that God the Son "became as we are in order that we might become as he is."

Monnica

Mother of Augustine of Hippo

Monnica, the mother of Augustine (see August 28) has long been regarded as a paragon of Christian motherhood. She was certainly a very loving and loyal wife and mother. The portrait we have of her in Augustine's writings is more than most Christian mothers dream of.

In more recent times some other aspects of her character have come into focus. Thanks to the Freudian psychologists and the Woman's Liberation movement, we can now view her in a new light. Considering Augustine's strong personality and virile interests she appears to have been at least an "adequate" mother. She had to struggle with a drinking problem of her own as well as with her husband's infidelity and violent temper. She was a very active participant in the "revolutionary" Christian movement. She was, of course, very much dedicated to her role as wife and mother, but she could hardly be called a "passive domestic." She was a most positive influence in her son's life, perhaps because she "led a life of her own." If one sees in motherhood constancy, affection, unselfishness, patience, wisdom, and integrity, then Monnica is a good example.

Almighty and everlasting God, who did enkindle the flame of your love in the heart of your servant Monica: Grant to us, your humble servants, the same faith and power of love; that, as we rejoice in her triumph, we may profit by her example; through Jesus Christ our Lord.

Gregory of Nazianzus

Bishop of Constantinople

A Great Model Pastor

Gregory was a bishop's son, well off financially, and educated at the very finest schools of his day, including the universities of Alexandria and Athens. Among his school comrades was Basil (see June 14), and when he finished school Gregory participated in Basil's pioneer monastic community on the island of Pontus. However, he had no intention at that time of entering the priesthood. Then his father called him home and virtually thrust holy orders upon him. Gregory took the priestly office very seriously and was terrified at having it foisted upon him. He fled back to Pontus and, by much prayer, fasting, and soul searching, became reconciled to this new vocation.

The ecclesiastical career thus launched was to become a most distinguished one. Gregory was soon elected Bishop of Sasina. He was one of the most effective preachers against the Arian heresy.

The imperial city, Constantinople, was in the hands of the Arians and was ruled by the Arian emperor, Valens. When the emperor died in battle and the city was reopened to orthodox Christians, Gregory was the first bishop to enter the city. He was chiefly responsible for the reconversion of the city and he eventually became its bishop. He skillfully led his people through a time of violence and discord in the church, avoiding controversy over all but the most essential issues. "It is unwise for those who walk the high tight rope to lean to either side."

Dunstan

Archbishop of Canterbury

Reformer of State and Church

By the tenth century England was exhausted through invasion and tribal warfare. Monastic life had degenerated, with few monks and fewer still who took seriously their vows and rules. Then a young monk appeared on the scene at Glastonbury monastery. His name was Dunstan and he was inspired to rejuvenate the lagging monasteries and revive the weary country. At Glastonbury he was instrumental in instituting the rigorous Benedictine Rule, and he got the scriptorium, a center for serious study, reopened. Finally, he was elected Abbot.

As the good reputation of Glastonbury spread, the new Abbot was inevitably drawn into politics. He served as Royal Treasurer to King Edred and under King Edgar he became, successively, Bishop of Worcester, of London, and finally Archbishop of Canterbury.

As Archbishop, Dunstan put all his resources to work to strengthen and rebuild the decaying and war-ravaged church in England. Among a people who knew almost nothing save the art of warfare, he preached and taught the skills of peace, industry, and learning. Schools, monasteries, farms, and shops reappeared on the English countryside. Slavery, debauchery, and concubinage waned. The authority of the church was respected and England enjoyed a peace and unity unknown before.

O God, we thank you for the ministry of Dunstan.

Alcuin

Deacon, and Abbot of Tours

Inspirer of the Carolingian Renaissance

A breath of fresh air swept across Western Europe in what we call the "Age of Charlemagne." There was relative peace, security, and prosperity. Learning and the arts revived. The leading spirit of this renaissance was Alcuin of York.

Alcuin was the foremost teacher of his day. He revived "letters." Indeed, he is credited with the invention of the running script we use today. He was a competent theologian, poet, and author. He was a pioneer in conceiving the "idea of a university."

After serving for some years as Master of the Cathedral School in York, England, he traveled to Italy to study. There he met Charlemagne and they became fast friends. Alcuin served as royal tutor and as the great king's chief advisor in religious and educational matters. In 796 he became Abbot of the monastery at Tours, France, and there he founded a famous library and school. From there he exercised great influence in correcting misunderstandings of the Christian Faith and in discouraging practices which seemed inconsistent with this Faith, both in morals and in forms of worship.

We beseech you to shed upon your whole Church the bright beams of your light and peace, and help us to follow the good example of your servant Alcuin.

Jackson Kemper

Bishop

Missionary to the American Mid-West

The first Missionary Bishop of the Episcopal Church was also one of the greatest. A well-bred New Yorker and a pupil of Bishop Hobart (see September 12), his missionary activity began close to home, in Pennsylvania. He convinced the elderly Bishop White of Pennsylvania to visit the western portion of his diocese and then accompanied him on this journey.

The General Convention in 1835 consecrated him and sent him to the wilds of Indiana and Missouri. He found that there was but one church in each of these states. However, by 1850, thanks largely to the efforts of Jackson Kemper, both were flourishing dioceses with bishops of their own. Bishop Kemper toured the deep South, but the church was already prospering there. For "breathing space and room for expansion" he moved on into the Old Northwest. Wisconsin became his headquarters for the remainder of his life. He founded Nashotah House and from there he directed and conducted missionary activities in Iowa, Illinois, and Minnesota.

Here was a man of great vision and inexhaustible energy. More than any other single man, he built the Province of the Midwest.

Raise up, we pray you, in every land, heralds and evangelists of your kingdom, like your servant Jackson.

The Venerable Bede

Died May 25, 735

Priest, and Monk of Jarrow

Historian and Scholar

When the monks of Jarrow sang, "Lord, leave us not as orphans," it is said that Bede would often weep. As a child he was left orphaned in a dark, hostile, and dangerous land. He was cared for and reared by kindly monks. When he was but a youngster, plague struck the monastery, decimating it. The only surviving souls were Bede and the old Abbot. Bede naturally had a strong sense of the importance of community, of the fine line between life and death, and of our utter dependence upon the Creator.

He rarely ventured outside the walls of Jarrow monastery, yet his knowledge of theology, geography, and language was worthy of the most sophisticated of his time in Western Europe. He wrote a number of excellent books on various subjects, but he is best remembered for his *Ecclesiastical History of the English People*. This work has justly earned for him the title, "Father of English History." Unlike some of the careless historians of his day, he was meticulous in listing his authorities and sources. He takes care to separate known fact from hearsay, but his descriptions are lively and dramatic.

Bede thought of himself as a teacher, and he seems to have built most of his teaching around the Divine Offices which the monks read daily. It is altogether fitting that he was pronounced a "Doctor of the Church" by Pope Leo XIII. Bede's remains rest in Durham.

Augustine

Died May 26, 605

First Archbishop of Canterbury

Apostle to the Anglo-Saxons

Augustine and a group of monks were sent to Britain by Pope Gregory (see March 12) in 597. Three centuries prior to this Christianity had been introduced to the British Isles, during the Roman occupation (see June 22 and March 1 and 17). However, when the Roman forces withdrew, the pagan Anglo-Saxons invaded the Isles and forced the Christians to flee into the hills and forests of Wales, Scotland, and Ireland, or to face a tenuous existence in England. Augustine found that his task was not only to convert the Anglo-Saxons but also to reestablish contacts between the British (or "Celtic") and Roman Churches.

Now Augustine seems to have been a rather timid and reticent fellow who had accepted this assignment with something less than enthusiasm. He did not speak the Anglo-Saxon tongue and was terrified at the prospect of confronting these notorious savages. He was relieved and delighted upon landing in Britain to find that the Anglo-Saxon queen, Bertha, was already a Christian and that the king was not unfriendly. The latter, King Ethelbert, eventually was converted and in time most of his subjects followed suit. Augustine established his cathedral at Canterbury in Kent. This was destined to become the most important bishophric in England and the mother diocese of the Anglican Communion. Archbishops of Canterbury are still said to hold the "Chair of Augustine."

The Visitation of the Blessed Virgin Mary

Mary Visits Elizabeth, Mother of John the Baptist

According to Luke's Gospel, Mary, immediately after being told of the forthcoming birth of Jesus, went to visit her cousin, Elizabeth. Elizabeth was also pregnant and her child was to be John the Baptist. This famous visit was important for several reasons.

When Elizabeth saw Mary, the baby leaped in her womb, not an uncommon experience in pregnancy but in this case regarded as a supernatural occurrence, signifying little John's excitement at the presence of the Saviour whom he was to proclaim. Elizabeth was the first to recognize Mary as the Mother of the Lord, exclaiming "Blessed art thou among women and blessed is the fruit of thy womb!"

The moving and eloquent canticle, *Magnificat,* is recorded by Luke at this point. It is called the "Song of Mary" and although it could hardly have been a stenographers report of what the blessed Mother said at the time, it most surely reflects her sentiments and the kind of response she must have expressed.

Father in heaven, who chose in wondrous grace the blessed Virgin Mary to be the mother of your incarnate Son: Grant that, as we honor the exaltation of her lowliness, so we may follow the example of her humble obedience to your will; through Jesus Christ your Son our Lord, who now lives and reigns with you and the Holy Spirit, one God, in glory everlasting.

Justin

Martyr at Rome

Early Christian Apologist

An apologist is one who attempts to make clear the grounds for his belief or course of action, one who attempts to explain to others the truth and validity of what he stands for. Justin was such an apologist for the early church.

He was born in Samaria but was a gentile and a pagan. As a young man he engaged in a long struggle for truth and meaning. He was for a time a Stoic, later a Pythagorean, and then a Platonist. Finally, in the ancient "melting pot" of Ephesus, he embraced Christianity, which he continued to regard as the most sublime revelation of truth to his very death.

Eventually Justin went to Rome and there, for some fifteen years, he operated a Christian school. He was not exceptionally skilled in either philosophy or literature, nor was he very original, but he compiled in his *Apologies* the most convincing and most popular arguments for Christianity extant. His strong, clear Christian witness became more than the Roman authorities could bear. He was prosecuted for atheism and found guilty. He and a group of his disciples were scourged and beheaded.

Almighty God, who did give your servant Justin boldness to confess the Name of our Saviour Jesus Christ before the rulers of this world: Grant that we likewise may ever be ready to give a reason for the hope that is in us.

The Martyrs of Lyons

First Martyrs in France

Lyons in Gaul (France) was the scene of one of the most terrible persecutions the early church had to endure. The Christians there were accused, as elsewhere, of atheism, blasphemy, treason, sexual perversion, and cannibalism. The Governor, hoping to please the Emperor Marcus Aurelius, staged public trials which lasted for several days and in which the populace was stirred into a mad frenzy against the Christians. Many were imprisoned, tortured, and beaten to death. Their remains were thrown to the dogs.

Among those mentioned by name in Eusebius' moving account was Alexander, a physician who was publicly roasted. He professed Christ and, when asked what God's name was, he replied, "God has no name as men have." As he expired he pointed out to the pagans that they were the ones who consumed human flesh. There was Blandina, "a blessed woman" who, "like a noble athlete," endured days of excruciating torture, abuse, and humiliation, saying only, "I am a Christian woman and nothing wicked happens among us." She was gored to death by a bull in the arena. Then there was the notable citizen Attalus, the elderly Bishop Pothinus, a deacon from Vienna, Sanctus, and a lad of fifteen, Ponticus. These and many others were subjected to brutal horrors and torments and were finally killed. Undaunted, they passed out of this world joyfully and victoriously, witnesses to the only living Lord.

The Martyrs of Uganda

Martyrs of Modern Africa

Africa boasts the world's oldest Christian kingdom extant, Ethiopia, and also some of the newest Christian countries. Uganda in East Africa is one. A former British protectorate, it is now an independent republic and a part of the British Commonwealth.

Christianity was introduced to Uganda by Anglican and Roman Catholic missionaries in the nineteenth century. They were well received by the powerful King of Buganda, Mutesa. However, he was not converted, and he was succeeded by King Mwanga, a degenerate and perverse individual who sought a return to primitive animism. He expelled missionaries and began systematically terrorizing the native Christians. Many were flogged and mutilated. In 1884 three youths were burned to death for their faith. They were said to have approached martyrdom singing the favorite Swahili hymn, "Daily, daily sing the praises." We do not know how many Christians died in this persecution but, between May 25th and June 3rd, 1886, at least thirty-two were martyred, most of them on a great pyre at Namugongo.

Out of these afflictions, however, grew a strong indigenous church, a symbol of resurgent Christianity in Africa and of successful cooperation between Anglicans and Roman Catholics.

Grant us so to cherish the blessed Martyrs of Uganda that we may share their steadfast faith.

Boniface

Archbishop of Mainz

Missionary to Germany

One of the great achievements of the Anglo-Saxon Christians was the conversion of their cousins in Germany. The trail was blazed by Willibrord (see November 7) but the man to whom most credit is due was Boniface of Devonshire, England. His real name was Wynfrith. Boniface ("good deeds") was a nickname that stuck.

In spite of some disappointing efforts in Frisia (Holland), the missionary, Boniface, proceeded into the Germanic heartland. In Bavaria, Thuringia, and Hesse he won many converts to Christ. In an act of extraordinary boldness, he chopped down the sacred Oak of Thor at Geismar. With the felling of this tree, Germanic confidence in the old gods fell. From then on Boniface's work progressed rapidly. He soon organized eight German dioceses, founded the famous Abbey at Fulda, and was himself consecrated the first Archbishop of Mainz. Boniface always kept in close touch with England, writing many letters to friends at home who supplied him with books, vestments, and recruits for the work in Germany.

Still concerned about the Frisians with whom he had failed, Boniface made another effort to revive the church there. In this attempt he was slain by a mob of Frisian pagans near Utrecht.

Thank you for your servant Boniface.

Columba

Abbot of Iona

Apostle of Scotland

In the troubled and violent Dark Ages in Northern Europe monasteries served as inns, orphanages, centers of learning, and even as fortresses. The light of civilization flickered dimly and might have gone out altogether had it not been for these convent-shelters.

Columba, a stern and strong monk from Ireland, founded three such establishments. He founded the monasteries of Derry and Durrow on his native island, and Iona on the coast of Scotland. Iona was the center of operations for the conversion of the Scots and Picts and became the most famous religious house in Scotland. There Columba baptised Brude, King of the Picts, and later a King of the Scots came to this Abbot of the "Holy Isle" for baptism.

The historian Bede tells us that Columba led many to Christianity by his "preaching and example." He was much admired for his physical as well as spiritual prowess. He was a vigorous ascetic and was still quite active when he died, nearly eighty years old. The memory of Columba lives on in Scotland, and Iona, though desecrated during the Reformation, is today a Protestant religious community.

Almighty God, you did choose your servant Columba to be an apostle to the people of Scotland, to bring those who were wandering in darkness to your true light: Grant us to walk in that same light.

Ephrem of Edessa

Died June 10, 373

Deacon

Syrian Doctor of the Church

Christianity flourished early in Syria, and Antioch was a major center of the church. Although that land is today dominated by Moslems, the Syrian Orthodox Church still has well over a million members in the world. One of the great fathers of the church in Syria was Ephrem of Edessa.

Ephrem was the head of a very successful Christian school in Edessa, Syria. There he championed the Nicene faith, and in fact he may have been present in Nicaea for the famous council which met there in 325. He became well known for the austerity and sanctity of his life as well as for his learning. His writings are voluminous and include biblical commentaries, essays on dogma, history, and biography, as well as a host of hymns. Many of the latter have long been an integral part of Syrian Orthodox worship.

The Anglican Communion has long enjoyed warm and friendly relations with the Syrian Church. Ephrem's feast would seem an appropriate time to give thanks to God for this relationship and for the witness of the Syrian Christians today and through the ages.

Almighty God, who enriched your Church with the singular learning and holiness of your Deacon Ephrem: Grant us to hold fast the true doctrine of your Son our Saviour Jesus Christ, and to fashion our lives according to the same, to the glory of your great Name.

Barnabas

Apostle

Barnabas, a Jew from the island of Cyprus, was not one of the Twelve of our Lord's disciples. However, he may have been one of the Seventy. He came to be so closely associated with the early church that he is customarily called an "apostle."

When Barnabas joined the Christian church it was "for keeps," as he demonstrated when he sold his land and gave the proceeds to the "company of those who believed." It was Barnabas who discovered Paul and brought him into the Christian community. Paul and Barnabas became great friends. Together they nurtured the young church at Antioch. They went on missionary journeys together and seem to have been an impressive team. Both seem to have continued to hold secular employment for some time after taking up their ecclesiastical roles.

Barnabas was also a friend to Mark, the Evangelist (see April 25), and they did missionary work together. Barnabas is regarded as the founder of the church on his native Cyprus and is alleged to have been martyred at Salamis in A.D. 61.

O God, whose Son Jesus Christ has taught us that it is more blessed to give than to receive: Help us, by the example of your apostle and servant Barnabas, to be generous in our judgments and unselfish in our service; through Jesus Christ our Lord, who lives and reigns with you and the Holy Spirit, one God, now and for ever.

Basil the Great

Bishop of Caesarea

An Eastern Father of the Church

More than any other single man, Basil, Bishop of Caesarea in Cappadocia (modern central Turkey), was responsible for the shaping of the Eastern Church. He was handsome, brilliant, wealthy, and educated in the finest schools of his day. He did not turn from poverty of body or intellect to Christianity. He was a close friend of Gregory Nazianzus (see May 9) and his brother was Gregory of Nyssa (see March 9). He was an eloquent preacher and a most persuasive statesman. He was one of the key figures in the triumph of Christian orthodoxy over Arianism. He was a major contributor to the Divine Liturgy of the Eastern Church which bears his name. Early in his career he founded a monastery on the island of Pontus, and he put forward the monastic rule that still prevails in the Eastern Church.

Basil would accept no interpretation of the gospel that called for anything less than radical social action. He founded hospitals and organized a massive program for the relief of the poor, both of which were successful then and for many generations after his death. He called the rich Christians of his city "thieves," saying, "What other name does he deserve who, being able to clothe the naked, yet refuses? . . . The clothes you store away belong to the naked; the shoes that molder in your closet belong to those who have none. . . ."

Grant us to hold fast to Basil's faith.

Joseph Butler

Bishop of Durham

Scholar and Pastor

The English Church in the eighteenth century was besieged by Deists, Non-Conforming Evangelicals, and most of all by indifferent or lazy clergy of her own. Joseph Butler was an outstanding example of the "other side of the coin." Operating well within the structures and traditions of the Established Church, he forged a positive Christian apologetic which has outlived the attitudes of his opponents. He is credited with breaking the force of Deism in England, without compromising his reason, and with saving many from fanatic Evangelicalism, without surrendering his warmth, personal piety, or social concern. His masterpiece, the *Analogy of Religion,* is still considered one of the most reasoned and convincing defenses of Christian faith and ethic.

Butler first established a reputation as a preacher at the Rolls Chapel, London, where his famous *Fifteen Sermons* were delivered and published. He wrote the *Analogy of Religion* under very different circumstances, as rector of the small parish of Stanhope in the North of England. He was elected Bishop of Bristol and served most admirably in that post for twelve years before accepting the bishophric of Durham in which position he died. Bishop Butler was a great pastor, who served the minds as well as the bodies and spirits of his people.

We thank you for the teaching of your servant Joseph; may our witness be as faithful.

Bernard Mizeki

Died June 18, 1896

Martyr in Rhodesia

As a teenager Bernard Mizeki fled from the oppression of his native Portuguese East Africa, escaping to Capetown, South Africa. There he was educated, converted, and baptised by Anglican missionaries.

At age thirty he volunteered to serve as a teacher at a small pioneer mission in Mashonaland, Southern Rhodesia. There, in isolated and primitive Nhowa, he worked for five years, gaining many converts and breaking the spell that superstition and ignorance had for so long held over the people.

These were very troubled times in Rhodesia and missionaries were often regarded as the "stooges" of European imperialists. So it was with Bernard Mizeki. When a native uprising occurred in 1896 he was warned to flee, but, not regarding himself as an enemy of the natives, and not wishing to leave his recent converts, he remained. He was brutally stabbed to death. Afterwards his body, mysteriously, was never found. Today, a shrine at the sight of his martyrdom attracts many pilgrims.

Almighty God, by whose grace and power your holy martyr Bernard triumphed over suffering, and was faithful even to death: Grant us, who now remember him in thanksgiving, to be so faithful in our witness to you in this world, that we may receive with him the crown of everlasting life; through Jesus Christ our Lord, who lives and reigns with you and the Holy Spirit forever.

Robert Hunt

June 21, 1607

Priest

America's First Anglican Pastor

After much prayerful consideration, the Rev. Robert Hunt, Vicar of Heathfield, was chosen chaplain to the Virginia Company. Bravely and hopefully he left his wife and two small children behind and set out to make a new home for them in America. During the long voyage he "became so weak and sick that few expected his recovery." Yet he was continually leading in prayer, so much so that some "men of fashion" on board complained.

Finally, the colonists disembarked at what was to become Jamestown. Chaplain Hunt dedicated the spot to the glory of God and they "began thereon . . . in the name of God to raise a fortress." The first permanent building they erected was a church, but even before then they stretched a sail between the trees and under this primitive shelter, on June 21, 1607, Holy Communion was first celebrated in America.

According to Captain John Smith, Hunt was an honest and courageous clergyman who "with patience and godly exhortations quenched the flames of envy and dissention." Besides leading the colony in daily morning and evening prayer, he preached twice on Sundays, cared for the sick, buried the dead, and did as much labor as any man. During the first terrible "starving time" he found comfort and refreshment in his books. A few months later he "took sick" and died. Without his valiant spirit the colony might not have survived.

74

Alban

First Martyr of Britain

"In Britain's Isle was holy Alban born." Alban was a young pagan who lived in the Roman town of Verulamium (modern St. Albans, Hertfordshire, just north of London). During the persecution of Diocletian (some historians think Decius), he sheltered a Christian priest in his home. The priest converted and baptised him. Later, when Roman soldiers came to search the house, Alban hid the priest and disguised himself in the priest's cloak. He was dragged off to court. When it was discovered who he was and what he had done he was accused of harboring a rebelious and sacrilegious person. Alban then publicly confessed his faith in Jesus Christ, was scourged and, still persisting in his confession, was sentenced to death. The executioner refused to do his duty and he and the priest, whose names we do not know, soon became the second and third British martyrs.

Alban has always been highly honored among British Christians. St. Alban's Abbey was a great medieval monument to him and there his shrine still stands.

Almighty God, by whose grace and power your holy martyr Alban triumphed over suffering, and despised death: Grant, we beseech you, that enduring hardness, and waxing valiant in fight, we may with the noble army of martyrs receive the crown of everlasting life; through Jesus Christ our Lord.

The Nativity of John the Baptist

The Herald of the Christ

The prophet and forerunner of Jesus was his cousin, John, the only child of Elizabeth and Zechariah. He is sometimes called, "the last and the greatest of the prophets."

John lived very plainly, wearing "camel's hair and a leather girdle" and eating "locusts and wild honey." He preached repentance and called upon men to prepare for the coming of the Messiah. He baptised his followers to signify their repentance and new life. Hence he was called John the Baptist. Jesus himself was baptised by John in the River Jordan. John had many followers, at least some of whom became Christians. He preached strongly against the notorious sins of King Herod and was finally beheaded by the King at the request of his daughter Salome.

John figures prominently in the New Testament and Luke gives us an account of his nativity. His parents were elderly at the time of his birth. His father, a priest of the Temple in Jerusalem, was struck dumb in a vision foretelling John's birth and did not speak again until the baby was born. The magnificent canticle, *Benedictus* (Prayer Book, page 14), is attributed to Zechariah, the joyful father.

John is particularly remembered as a prophet during the Advent season and as the baptiser of Jesus during Epiphany.

Irenaeus

Bishop of Lyons

A Western Father of the Church

Scarcely had the blood of the Martyrs of Lyons (see June 2) dried before Irenaeus was consecrated Bishop of Lyons. He had narrowly escaped the persecution himself, being on church business in Rome at the time.

As a lad Irenaeus had learned the Christian faith at the knee of Polycarp (see February 23) in his native Smyrna. After a period of study in Rome he moved to Gaul (France) where he was elected bishop. He served Lyons in that capacity for a quarter of a century and during that time sufficiently influenced the whole church that he came to be regarded as one of the Fathers.

Irenaeus wrote a number of significant letters, an essay entitled "The Demonstration of Apostolic Preaching," and a major work *Against Heresies,* all in Greek. He was an avid student of the Holy Scriptures, a tireless pastor, and the first great theologian of the Western Church. He was a champion of orthodoxy against Gnosticism, a champion of episcopal polity and of the canonical Scriptures. Today's heirs of Irenaeus live the life of faith expounded in the church's doctrine, are loyal to their bishops and pastors, and diligently study the Holy Bible.

Almighty God, who did uphold your servant Irenaeus with strength to maintain the truth against every wind of vain doctrine: We beseech you to keep us steadfast in your true religion, and to walk in constancy.

Peter and Paul

Apostles and Martyrs

Peter and Paul are commemorated individually on January 18th and January 25th, respectively. However, following an ancient custom, we remember them together on this the presumed date of their martyrdom. Christian tradition has long held that these two stalwart leaders of the early church died together in the Neronian persecution of 64 A.D.

In so many ways Peter and Paul were very different from one another. Paul was a well educated and cosmopolitan Jew of the Diaspora, reared in the sophisticated city of Tarsus. Peter was an uneducated provincial and a fisherman. Peter was the more conservative of the two, as one might expect, and it is not surprising that they had strong differences of opinion. They were leaders of opposing points of view at the first church council in Jerusalem. However, their common commitment to Christ and his church proved far stronger than their individual points of view. In the risen Lord they found reconciliation and, fittingly, they died together, crucified as he had been.

Nero thought he had found "the final solution to the Christian problem." On the contrary, the church was "nourished by the blood of her martyrs" and it was Christ, the Lord of Peter and Paul, who was ultimately to triumph, not Nero.

Grant that your household the Church may be instructed by their teaching and example.

Independence Day

The American Nation is Founded

Christians have long championed justice and sound government, and opposed the twin evils of oppression on the one hand and anarchy on the other. When America won her independence and founded a new nation on this continent she was seen by many as stepping boldly away from oppression but stopping short of anarchy. Many Anglican churchmen led in this struggle and on this day it seems appropriate to mention a few. Richard Henry Lee first proposed the Declaration of Independence and Thomas Jefferson and Benjamin Franklin contributed to the writing of it. George Washington, "on whose character the Revolution rested," was a staunch Episcopal Churchman, as was James Madison, the "Father of the Constitution," and John Paul Jones, the "Father of the American Navy."

Many people are under the impression that our church benefited from its special relationship to the English State in colonial America. That was hardly the case. The controls imposed by the government hamstrung the church and seriously hampered her natural growth in the New World. No people had more cause to rejoice over "the inestimable blessings of religious and civil liberty" than our Anglican ancestors at the end of the American Revolution. At last we could have American bishops and an American version of the Book of Common Prayer.

God bless our native land.

Benedict of Nursia

Died July 11, c.540

Abbot of Monte Cassino

Founder of Western Monasticism

The serious breakdown of society and authority in 5th century Europe led to the downfall of many men and caused many others simply to run away from society and hide as hermits, hating and despairing of mankind. Benedict of Nursia rejected both of these alternatives. Instead he entered on a brave new venture. At Subiaco, and later at Monte Cassino (both in Italy), he founded the first monastic communities of Western Europe.

He drafted a firm but reasonable "Rule" (i.e. constitution) for these communities. He was never ordained and his communities were composed only of laymen at first. Their lives centered around the daily offices. When they were not praying and studying scripture, they were engaged in manual labor and in works of charity. Like the early Christians, they held all property in common.

Benedict attracted little attention in his own lifetime, but after his death, as the monasteries grew and spread so did his fame. The "Benedictine" monasteries became little islands where a man could still learn to love God and his fellow man and truly practice the Christian religion in his whole life. These communities operated schools, orphanages, hospitals, and assumed many of the functions of state.

Benedictine monks were largely responsible for the conversion and civilization of England. Westminster Abbey was for centuries a Benedictine house. Nashdom Abbey is its modern center in England.

William White

Died July 17, 1836

Bishop of Pennsylvania

First Presiding Bishop of the American Church

At the conclusion of the American Revolution there was grave concern among churchmen, many of whom had stoutly supported the Revolution, that the Anglican Church might succumb as a disastrous side-effect of that Revolution.

One of the most tireless and effective workers for an autonomous Episcopal Church in the U.S.A. was the Rev. William White, Rector of Christ Church, Philadelphia, and former Chaplain of the Continental Congress. Appropriately, he became the first American bishop consecrated in the English line. He was a quiet and scholarly man and an intimate friend of some of the prominent leaders of both America and England. As a clergyman in Philadelphia he had exhibited an unusual sensitivity for the poor, the unfortunate, and those who were in trouble. He was president of the Philadelphia Dispensary, which supplied medical aid to the poor; of the Pennsylvania Institute for the Deaf and Dumb; and of the Philadelphia Society for Alleviating the Miseries of Public Prisons. He was concerned about religious education, was instrumental in the founding of the first Episcopal Sunday School in America.

On February 4th, 1787, in Lambeth Chapel, London, William White was consecrated by the Archbishop of Canterbury, John Moore, and two other bishops. He returned immediately to America and became the first Presiding Bishop of the Episcopal Church in the U.S.A.

Mary Magdalene

A Disciple of the Lord

Mary of Magdala (Magdalene) was one of several women of ill repute whose lives were radically changed by Jesus. She was said to be "possessed by seven demons" and was considered "lost," beyond redemption, by the authorities of that time. The scriptures are not explicit about the nature of her many sins, but it is made very clear that Jesus gave her the will and power to abandon them. Nevertheless, the authorities were not impressed and Jesus seems to have been criticized for keeping the company of such people.

Tradition has held that she was a very emotional person and our English word "maudlin" derives from her name. Mary of Magdala followed Jesus into Galilee and helped care for him and the disciples there. She witnessed the Lord's suffering on the cross. She took oil to anoint his entombed body and therefore she is often represented with a jar of ointment. Her tearful reaction finding an empty tomb is still a favorite line to many faithful, "They have taken my Lord away and I do not know where they have laid him." When the Lord appeared and called her name, "Mary," she recognized him and exclaimed, "My Master!" She was the first to see the risen Lord.

Mercifully grant that by your grace we may be healed of all our infirmities and, like your servant Mary, be restored to health of body and of mind.

Thomas a Kempis

Died July 24, 1471

Priest

Scholar, Pastor, and Author

Few if any books, save the Holy Scriptures, have had as profound an effect on Christian piety as *The Imitation of Christ* by Thomas a Kempis. The author eloquently advances the notion that, "Whosoever would fully and feelingly understand the words of Christ, must endeavor to conform his life wholly to the life of Christ." The theme of the book is set forth in its first sentence, a quotation from the Gospel of John. " 'He that followeth me walketh not in darkness,' saith the Lord." The last part of the book contains a form of self-examination for use before receiving Holy Communion. Many Christians, both Catholic and Protestant, still find this a most helpful guide in their devotional lives.

Thomas led a relatively quiet and unspectacular life as a priest at the Augustinian convent of Mount St. Agnes, near Zwolle, in the Netherlands. He was born and named Thomas Hammerken at Kempen, a small town near Dusseldorf in Germany. He was educated by the Brothers of the Common Life, one of the most famous teaching orders of that time. He pursued a scholarly and contemplative life, but became famous as a preacher, and his advice and counsel was often sought by men and women of all walks of life.

Grant that we may follow the good example of your servant Thomas, and hold fast the faith.

Apostle of the Lord

James and his brother, John, were young fishermen, the sons of Zebedee and his wife, Salome. Salome was a sister of Mary, the Mother of our Lord, making James a first cousin to Jesus.

The fishing trade, then as now, was a tough one, and it is not surprising that James and his brother were high-spirited and hot tempered young men. They were called "Boanerges," i.e. "Sons of Thunder." Jesus seems to have been particularly fond of these somewhat rowdy companions. They were part of the "inner circle" that was present at the Transfiguration. They certainly must have aggravated the other disciples when they asked to sit on either side of the Lord when he came into his Kingdom. Furthermore, this request showed little insight into Jesus' teaching. Yet Jesus was very mild in his rebuke of them and used the occasion to try to prepare them for the suffering which was to come.

This well loved and promising disciple, James, was to have but a brief ministry. He was soon brutally martyred by Herod the king.

Almighty God, who gave to your apostle Saint James a ready will to obey the calling of your Son, and strength to suffer for his Name: Mercifully grant that no worldly affections may draw our hearts away from steadfast devotion to his service; through Jesus Christ your Son our Lord, who lives and reigns with you and the Holy Spirit, one God, now and evermore.

Anne and Joachim

The Parents of the Blessed Virgin Mary

We have little historical information concerning the parents of Mary, although we have a wealth of legend and tradition. Anne has long been honored in the naming of countless churches, hospitals, guilds, and various charitable institutions. Her feast is universally celebrated and she is the patroness of Brittany.

Joachim, husband of Anne and father of Mary, has received less attention. We know nothing about him, save his name, and even that is controversial.

Perhaps this date is an appropriate time to reflect on the importance of parenthood. What kind of influence are we having on our children? Do our lives reflect the best in the care and training we received from our parents? All we really know about Anne and Joachim is an inference from the kind of daughter they reared.

O almighty God, who has called us to faith in you, and has compassed us about with so great a cloud of witnesses: Grant that we, encouraged by the good examples of your Saints, and especially of your servants Anne and Joachim, may persevere in running the race that is set before us, until at length, through your mercy, we with them attain to your eternal joy; through him who is the author and finisher of our faith, your Son Jesus Christ our Lord.

William Reed Huntington

Died July 27, 1909

Priest

19th Century Church Leader

If any one man could be seen as typifying the spirit of the Episcopal Church in the 19th century, it would probably be W. R. Huntington, a priest from Massachusetts who was Rector of Grace Church, New York City, for over twenty-five years. Dr. Huntington was a leader in the House of Deputies for thirteen consecutive General Conventions (1871-1907). He was one of the designers of the Prayer Book revision of 1892 and he led the movement to revive the order of deaconesses in the Episcopal Church.

He profoundly influenced the course of ecumenical relations with his book, *The Church Idea—An Essay Toward Unity,* which first advanced the concept of a reunion of the universal church on the basis of mutual acceptance of the scriptures, the creeds, the sacraments, and the historic episcopate. This became the famous "Lambeth Quadrilateral" and the foundation on which Anglican discussions of unity with other Christian bodies have taken place the world over.

Dr. Huntington, living in the time of the "Monkey Trial" and other crises which pitted religion and science against one another, said, "the theologians and naturalists are allies. Truth is truth, however and whencesoever obtained, and we can never have occasion to be either afraid of it or unthankful for it."

Inspire us, Lord, as you did your servant William.

Mary and Martha of Bethany

Companions of the Lord

Mary and Martha lived with their brother, Lazarus, at Bethany, a village not far from Jerusalem. They seem to have been very sensitive and compassionate girls and gladly entertained Jesus and the disciples in their home. Mary, on one occasion, anointed Jesus' feet with expensive oil in an outpouring of emotion and love which drew criticism from some of the disciples. To them this act seemed sentimental and wasteful. On another occasion Mary was criticised by Martha for neglecting her household duties in order to "sit at the feet of Jesus." On both of these occasions Jesus came to the defense of Mary.

It was Martha who met Jesus when he came to her family on the death of Lazarus and who confidently testified that had he been there Lazarus would not have died. It was to Martha that Jesus said, "I am the resurrection and the life. . . ."

Jesus had no more loyal and generous followers than Mary and Martha of Bethany. Their examples of devotion and fidelity have inspired Christian women for generations.

Almighty and everlasting God, who enkindled the flame of your love in the heart of your servants Mary and Martha: Grant to us, your humble servants, a like faith and power of love; that, as we rejoice in their triumph, we may profit by their examples; through Jesus Christ our Lord.

William Wilberforce

Member of Parliament

Christian Statesman

So often a devout and well-informed layman is a far more effective servant of the church than a professional clergyman. William Wilberforce of Hull, England, is an excellent example. He was a devoted student of the New Testament and a strong churchman. He was educated at Cambridge University and traveled widely. A deep concern for the Lord and his work led Wilberforce to the "brink of Holy Orders." However, under the influence of John Newton, he decided that he could better serve Christ as a politician.

For over fifty years, William Wilberforce served the church, his country, and the world as a Member of Parliament and an eloquent spokesman for Christian values and ethics. He is probably best remembered for his efforts to end slavery in the British Empire. The crowning achievement of his legislative career, the Emancipation Act of 1833, was passed one month after his death. He also championed the cause of Catholic Emancipation in the British Isles, of English missions in India, of parliamentary reform, and of judicial and prison reform. He wrote *A Practical View of the Prevailing Religious System of Professed Christians,* which was widely read both in England and on the continent, and which significantly influenced religious and political thinking in his day.

May we also, like William, defend the poor.

Joseph of Arimathaea

The Gentleman in Whose Tomb Jesus was Buried

Joseph was a wealthy and pious Jew and a member of the Sanhedrin, the Council which tried Jesus. The Gospel according to Luke indicates that Joseph did not consent to the decision that Jesus be crucified, and other scriptures suggest that he may have absented himself from the trial. It is believed that he was a "secret" disciple of Christ, like Nicodemus.

After the crucifixion, Joseph displayed considerable courage in going to Pilate and asking for the privilege of burying the body of Jesus with proper care and ceremony. In fact, Joseph reverently laid the body of Jesus in the fine tomb he had prepared for himself. John's Gospel indicates that Nicodemus helped Joseph prepare the body for burial. Looking back today, being aware of the resurrection, we tend not to see just how loyal, generous, and, indeed, pathetic this gesture must have been.

There is a charming medieval legend that Joseph of Arimathaea came to England and founded Glastonbury Abbey of Arthurian fame. This may, in part, account for his continued popularity among English Christians.

O merciful God, by whose servant Joseph the body of our Lord and Saviour was committed to the grave with reverence and godly fear: Grant, we beseech you, to your faithful people grace and courage to serve and love Jesus with unfeigned devotion all the days of their life; through the same Jesus Christ our Lord.

Dominic

Friar

Orthodox Reformer in the Middle Ages

The church has often been tempted to deal harshly and angrily with heresy and sometimes to defeat her own purposes in so doing, betraying the Lord's own teaching. This seemed to be the case in the crusade against the Albigensian heretics. Dominic, a learned and pious Spanish aristocrat, became deeply concerned about the situation and founded an Order of Preachers whose special task was to combat heresy with sound learning and intelligent preaching, rather than with force of arms. Members of this order came to be called "Dominicans," or in England, "Blackfriars," because of their black habit.

The Dominicans produced some of the greatest scholars and teachers of medieval Europe, including Albertus Magnus and Thomas Aquinas. They contributed significantly to the rise of the universities.

Dominic was a prodigious organizer and designed for his order a form of representative government, unique among monastic orders of his day. Dominic's god-son, Simon de Montfort, became a powerful leader among the English barons, and the Angevin kings of England favored the Dominicans. Therefore, Dominic and his Order of Preachers, seems to have contributed to the development of English Parliamentary government.

Sadly, the Order eventually became guilty of the very sins it was founded to oppose, associating itself with the Spanish Inquisition and with the Conquistadores.

The Transfiguration of our Lord Jesus Christ

A Marvelous Revelation to Three Companions of Jesus

Jesus had been seen by thousands, had taught and ministered to many, and was known intimately by a few. He was a very perplexing young man, especially to those who knew him best. He spoke as one with authority and he healed many. Who was he? Was he the Messiah? Was he even more?

Prior to his terrible humiliation and suffering he called three of his closest friends, Peter, James, and John, aside and it was revealed to them who he was. Moses and Elijah were seen speaking with him as one whom they knew, and the voice of the Father was heard to proclaim, "This is my beloved Son in whom I am well pleased." Jesus' relationship to the Old Testament prophets and his Divine Sonship were thus indicated to these three disciples. His face shone with a glorious light and they were astonished, falling on their faces and glorifying God.

Most of the world was by no means ready for this revelation. Indeed, the first reaction of the three disciples indicated that they had very little comprehension of what Jesus was about. The days ahead would clarify much. Yet, even today we stand before his glory astonished, puzzled, and bungling in our response to him.

O God, mercifully deliver us from the disquiet of this world.

John Mason Neale

Died August 7, 1866

Priest

Scholar of the Catholic Revival in the Church of England

The 19th century witnessed a reawakening of the Catholic spirit of the Church of England and in America. John Mason Neale was one of the prominent leaders in this revival. He was an eminent scholar of history and language, educated at Cambridge University and for twenty years the Warden of Sacksville College, East Grinsted.

He was a patient, modest, and devoted priest. He founded the Sisterhood of St. Margaret, a teaching and nursing order for women, and he weathered the storm of protests which arose over the establishment of it.

Neale was one of the most important hymn writers of the 19th century. *The Hymnal 1940* contains thirty-nine hymns either written or translated by him. Among these are such popular ones as, "Good Christian men rejoice," "All glory, laud, and honor," "Come ye faithful, raise the strain," and "Christ is made the sure foundation."

Always concerned about the education of children, Neale wrote numerous children's books. On the heavier side, some of his most impressive publications were *Commentary on the Psalms* (four volumes, 1864-1870) and *History of the Holy Eastern Church* (five volumes, 1847-1873). John Mason Neale awakened the minds of English and American Christians to the vast depth and breadth of their heritage.

Laurence

Deacon

Roman Martyr

One of the ancient and sacred duties of a deacon is to distribute food and to care for the poor. Laurence was one deacon who certainly took that assignment seriously. He was the trusted "right hand man" of Bishop Sixtus II of Rome. When the Emperor, Valerian, had Bishop Sixtus jailed, the Bishop entrusted the whole treasury of the Church in Rome to Deacon Laurence. Laurence gave it all to the poor and sick. When Valerian learned that Laurence had been given the treasury of the church, he hauled the deacon into court and demanded that he turn over that treasury—the funds of an illegal organization. Laurence responded by assembling a mob of infirm and impoverished persons and presenting them to the ruler, saying, "These are the treasure of the Church!" Valerian was greatly angered by this and had Laurence publicly executed. Tradition says that he was roasted alive, slowly, on a skewer. We have no nobler testimony to the faith and character of the 3rd century Christian Church than that of Laurence, Deacon and Martyr.

Almighty God, by whose grace and power your holy Deacon and martyr Laurence triumphed over suffering, and despised death: Grant, we beseech you, that enduring hardiness, and waxing valiant in fight, we may with the noble army of martyrs receive the crown of everlasting life; through Jesus Christ our Lord.

Clare of Assisi

Died August 11, 1253

Founder of the Poor Clares

Clare, the daughter of a noble Italian family, was very deeply touched by the teaching of Francis of Assisi. She refused two proffered marriages and when eighteen years old joined a convent of Benedictine nuns. Later, her sister, and finally her widowed mother, joined her in this convent. Then, with the help of Francis himself, these three founded the first Franciscan community for women. It was located at St. Damian's Church in Assisi. The community grew and flourished. There the "Poor Ladies," or "Poor Clares" as they came to be called, observed the same strict rules of poverty, humility, and devotion that the male Franciscans observed.

Filled with evangelical fervor and compassion for the souls of her little flock, Clare became a model abbess. For forty years she wisely and firmly led the community and oversaw the founding of similar communities throughout Europe. No one ever better personified the Franciscan ideal of renunciation for Christ's sake.

There is today an Anglican community of Poor Clares at Oxford, England, and one on Long Island, New York.

O God of mercy, enlighten the hearts of your faithful people, and grant us after the example of your servant Clare, not to mind earthly things, but to love things heavenly; through Jesus Christ our Lord.

Hippolytus

Bishop and Martyr

Early Leader of the Church in Rome

Not all great men are well remembered. Hippolytus, though one of the foremost leaders of the early church in Western Europe, was virtually forgotten in the Middle Ages. In relatively modern times his writings have been rediscovered and have once again exerted significant influence in the church.

His most famous books are *A Refutation of Heresies* and *The Apostolic Tradition*. The former is a well-reasoned and highly sophisticated series of arguments against some of the important religious errors of the 2nd and 3rd centuries. The latter is of more concrete nature, dealing with the organization and worship of the early church. It has been an invaluable document in modern liturgical renewal.

As an outspoken and effective leader in the Church in Rome, Hippolytus inevitably came into conflict with the authorities. He was exiled to Sardinia where he was forced to work in the quaries. He died there, presumably of maltreatment.

O God, who has enlightened your Church by the teaching of your servant Hippolytus: Enrich us evermore, we beseech you, with your heavenly grace, and raise up faithful witnesses who by their life and doctrine will set forth the truth of your salvation; through Jesus Christ our Lord.

Jeremy Taylor

Died August 14, 1667

Bishop of Down, Connor, and Dromore

Anglican Stalwart in Troubled Times

When the times are very troubled, learning and moderation are rarely regarded as virtues. Jeremy Taylor was a superb scholar and a man of deep spiritual insight. His learning, piety, and good advice gained him little popularity or peace in 17th century Britain.

Taylor's writings, however, have stood the test of time. His *Holy Living and Holy Dying* is a masterpiece of devotional prose and a gem of Christian wisdom, characteristic of the finest in Anglican spirituality. It stresses balance and moderation and insists on the discipline and good order in religion.

Taylor was a graduate of Cambridge University, a professor at Oxford, and a close friend of many of the religious and political leaders of his day. He served for a time as a chaplain to King Charles I and when the Puritan revolution errupted he was loyal to his king and church. For this he was imprisoned and forced into seclusion for a time. It was then that he did much of his writing.

When the kingdom and church were restored in 1660, Taylor's loyalty was lavishly rewarded. He was made Bishop of Down and Connor and vice-chancellor of Dublin University. There he spent the last years of his life, trying to steer a straight course through Ireland's violent Roman Catholic and Presbyterian confrontations.

Mary

Mother of our Lord

The Mother of our Lord is certainly the most remembered and most important of the saints, considering her very special relationship to him. Early in Christian history, when some men denied that Jesus Christ was truly a man, Christians pointed to the fact that he was born of a woman and inserted the phrase "born of the Virgin Mary" into the creed to emphasize Jesus' humanity. Later, when some other men denied that Jesus was God the Son, Greek Christians began calling Mary "Theotokos," i.e. "Bearer of God," to emphasize Jesus' true Godship. One's understanding of Christ governs one's understanding of Mary and vice versa.

Mary is often seen as representative of the church, the special vehicle or bearer of God to mankind. She is seen as the ideal mother who patiently cared for her little son and quietly accepted the highly unusual circumstances of his birth, life, death, and resurrection. In the Daily Offices, the church continually remembers her in the canticle attributed to her by Luke, the "Magnificat." She is particularly honored on five special feasts in the Christian Year. Perhaps her cousin, Elizabeth, best summed up the feeling of the faithful towards Mary when she said, "Blessed is she who believed that there would be a fulfillment of what was spoken to her from the Lord."

* *Purification, February, 2; Annunciation, March 25; Visitation, May 31; Nativity of our Lord, December 25.*

William Porcher Dubose

Died August 18, 1918

Priest

American Theologian

A century ago in an obscure corner of Southern Appalachia there lived and died a man who has been acclaimed "the only important creative theologian that the Episcopal Church in the United States has produced." He lived a life which, had any one less than he lived it, would have been called tragic. Born and reared in a prominent South Carolina family, he graduated from the Citadel and from the University of Virginia and served with some distinction as a Confederate line officer. However, in the Civil War and its aftermath he lost his wealth, his health, his wife, and finally his little son. In the meantime he had received Holy Orders and accepted a call as chaplain to the small Episcopal University at Sewanee, Tennessee. There he founded a School of Theology which still survives and there he did his greatest work.

His writings, *The Soteriology of the New Testament, The Gospel in the Gospels, High Priesthood and Sacrifice,* and other books, although applauded in England, were ill-received in his native land. While Oxford dons were calling him "the wisest writer on both sides of the Atlantic," W. P. DuBose was being threatened with a heresy trial at home. He died without wealth or fame, but he had sung "the Lord's song in a strange land" and, as a later biographer was to observe, he was a "live voice in an age of many echoes."

Bernard

Abbot of Clairvaux

Christian Leader in the Middle Ages

Though his body was meager and emaciated from strict monastic practices, the figure of Bernard of Clairvaux towered over the 12th century church like a colossus. This bold and forthright monk from Southern France, the Abbot of Clairvaux, tutored by the devout and wise Englishman, Stephen Harding, was the most eloquent and effective leader of both church and state in his generation. Bernard traveled widely, writing and speaking against the Albigensian heresy, against the Moslem invasion of the Christian East, and against the Christian mistreatment of Jews. He was drawn into every major international conflict of his day, including disputed Papal elections and the disastrous Second Crusade. But his chief concern was for the renewal of the church.

Bernard supervised the founding of at least sixty new monasteries. He taught absolute devotion to Christ and to the mission of his body, the church. His popular treatise *On the Love of God* still speaks clearly to those who read it. He lamented the indolence and vain luxury of many of the church's leaders, writing, "The church is resplendent in her walls, beggarly in her poor. She clothes her stones in gold, and leaves her sons naked!"

Almighty and everlasting God, who did enkindle the flame of your love in the heart of your servant Bernard: Grant to us, your humble servants, the same faith and power of love.

Bartholomew

Apostle of the Lord

We know very little of Bartholomew, even his name is something of a mystery. Bartholomew is a patronymic meaning "Son of Tolmai." He is mentioned only in the Synoptic Gospels (Matthew, Mark, and Luke) but he is generally believed to be the same person as Nathanael in John's Gospel.

He is credited by several reliable historical sources with writing a gospel, but the Gospel according to Bartholomew is lost today. Tradition holds that he traveled to India and this is certainly not inconceivable. He is regarded as the founder of the Church in Armenia and may have been martyred there. An ancient tradition maintains that he was flayed alive at Albanopolis, Armenia, by the authorities as a consequence of his evangelistic work.

Almighty and everlasting God, who gave to your apostle Bartholomew grace truly to believe and to preach your Word: Grant, we pray, that your Church may love the Word which he believed, and both preach it and obey it; through Jesus Christ our Lord, who lives and reigns with you and the Holy Spirit, one God, now and ever.

Note: Both *Forward Day by Day* and *Response* follow the new "Church Year," as an integral part of their devotional format.

Louis

King of France

Christian Monarch

In fiction and fancy King Louis IX of France is the "knight in shining armour" who gallantly led the French army in the Crusades. This idea of Louis is true, but this image emerged from a man of deep conviction and rigorous self-discipline.

Louis is best remembered in France as a peace-maker and law-giver. He curbed the private feudal warfare that had for years ravaged France and significantly reformed the taxing and judicial systems of the kingdom. He had a good sense of justice and fairness and tried to see that every man, peasant or prince, got his "day in court."

Strong in the Christian faith, he was a staunch opponent of the Albigensian heresy in France, but he was no bigot. He never made unreasonable demands on his enemies. Even the Arabs admired him, and his traditional enemies at home, the English, respected him so much that they asked him to arbitrate in their disputes among themselves.

Louis was a patron of learning and the arts. He was one of the founders of the University of Paris (the Sorbonne) and the grand cathedrals of Amiens, Bourges, and Chartres were largely built during his reign and with his patronage. Certainly the medieval ideal of Christian kingship was realized in the person of Louis IX.

Augustine

Died August 28, 430

Bishop of Hippo

Church Father

Augustine (not to be confused with Augustine of Canterbury) would be very much at home with some of today's collegians. He was reared in a "half-Christian" home which he left in search of truth. He "co-habitated" with a girl whom he was always to love but never to formally marry. She bore him a son who was the "apple of his eye." Augustine seriously sought the counsel of astrologers and all kinds of spiritual advisors and philosophers. He was a sincere Manichaean and, later, a convinced Platonist. Finally, under the influence of Ambrose, the great old Bishop of Milan, Augustine turned to "the Man from Galilee."

With the possible exception of Paul of Tarsus, no one has affected the Christian tradition, way of life, and thought, as profoundly as Augustine.

His autobiography, *Confessions,* his treatise, *On the Trinity,* and his famous essays, *On the City of God,* remain classics of Christian literature second only to the scripture itself. Much of modern Catholic and Protestant theology and practice derives from his original work.

Augustine eventually entered the priesthood and later was consecrated Bishop of Hippo in North Africa. He witnessed the sack of the city of Rome by Alaric, and as he lay on his deathbed Vandals were assaulting his own city of Hippo.

Help us to follow Augustine's example.

Aidan

Died August 31, 651

Bishop of Lindisfarne

Apostle of Northern England

It has often been observed that "actions speak louder than words" and that the best kind of Christian evangelism is that which proceeds from godly and charitable living. Aidan provides us with an example of just that.

Trained at Iona, Scotland's "Holy Isle," Aidan was already revered as a compassionate and well learned monk, when King Oswald of Northumbria invited him to come and help with the evangelization of Northern England. Aidan joyfully responded and began the work by founding a monastery on the Island of Lindisfarne. This monastery soon became a center for missionary and charitable activities throughout England and Scotland. The monks of Lindisfarne followed the old Celtic rites and practices, but Aidan traveled widely on the Continent and was able to familiarize them somewhat with the practices of the Roman Church, thus preparing his people for things to come.

Aidan trained a whole generation of Christian leaders for the English Church. Included among them were numerous bishops and saints. Perhaps the highest compliment paid to Aidan was that of the Venerable Bede who wrote that Aidan "taught no otherwise than he and his followers lived; for he neither sought nor loved anything of this world, but delighted in distributing to the poor whatsoever was given him by the kings or rich men of the world."

The Martyrs of New Guinea

Witnesses in World War II

New Guinea was the scene of much suffering when the Japanese invaded in 1942, especially among Christians there. Many European clergy and missionaries of other denominations had been withdrawn, had chosen to leave, or been forced to leave before the invasion. The Anglican Bishop of New Guinea, Philip Strong, issued this compelling message to his clergy: "We must endeavour to carry on or work. . . . God expects this of us. The church at home, which sent us out, will surely expect it of us. The universal church expects it of us. . . . The people whom we serve expect it of us. We could never hold up our faces again if, for our own safety, we all forsook him and fled, when the shadows of the passion began to gather around him in his spiritual and mystical body, the Church in Papua."

They stayed. Almost immediately there were arrests. Eight clergymen and two laymen were executed, "as an example." It was an example, indeed, and one which is well remembered, especially on September 2 in Australia and Indonesia. It was only the beginning of suffering and persecution which the young Church in New Guinea endured. It was the testing, the baptism in blood, which proved the metal of that young and vigorous part of Christ's Body.

Grant us, too, the courage to witness to our faith.

104

John Henry Hobart

Died September 12, 1830

Bishop of New York

American Church Leader

Bishop Hobart, always a powerhouse of energy, was one of the most capable and effective leaders of any sort in America in the early 19th century. A native of Philadelphia, he was educated and taught at Princeton University prior to entering the Christian priesthood. After serving for sometime as Rector of Trinity Church, New York, he was elected Bishop of New York in 1811. Always full of vigor and excitement, he took the lackadaisical and self-satisfied diocese and transformed it into a dynamic and effective center of American church life.

Hobart was a tireless traveler, lecturer, and author, as well as being a staunch advocate of Episcopal polity and the *Book of Common Prayer*. He organized one of the most impressive missionary efforts the American Church has ever seen. Episcopal Churches began springing up in Western New York and among the American Indians, thanks largely to his work and inspiration. Always an educator, Hobart was largely responsible for the success of the college which bears his name today in Geneva, New York, and for the General Theological Seminary in New York City.

But above all, John Henry Hobart was a well loved and loving bishop, highly personable and always accessible. He set an example for the new American episcopate which is still worthy of emulation today.

We thank you for your servant John, faithful steward.

Cyprian

Died September 13, 258

Bishop of Carthage

Theologian, Pastor, and Martyr

Cyprian was a respected attorney of Carthage who converted to Christianity in middle age. He had been baptized only two years before he was consecrated Bishop of Carthage. When the Decian persecution broke out he fled under duress, but retained the respect of his flock, continuing to correspond with those who were riding out the persecution in the city. When the persecution subsided Cyprian returned to carefully and firmly rebuild the diocese.

When a plague broke out in 252 he quickly mobilized the church to help those in need and spent countless hours personally ministering to the sick of the city. This did not prevent public opinion and the authorities from blaming the plague on the "impious Christians." Soon there was another persecution. This time under the Emperor Valerian, and this time Bishop Cyprian chose to stay in the city. He was arrested and exiled for a time, then tried and finally executed. At the trial, Cyprian the lawyer clearly showed through in his deportment and courtesy before the pro-consul. He never displayed any hostility towards the court at all and he even left a generous tip for the executioner who chopped off his head.

Cyprian wrote a number of short treatises on Christian living, all of which show a profound understanding of human nature. He was a moderate and compassionate pastor and an example to his flock.

Holy Cross Day

The Exaltation of the Cross of Christ

"I, if I be lifted up, will draw all men unto me." It seemed in the 4th century that these words of Jesus were swiftly being fulfilled. Christianity had swept over the known, civilized world. A Christian Emperor now reigned from the throne of the Caesars and it was he, Constantine the Great, who, on this day in 335 A.D., dedicated the Church of the Holy Sepulcre in Jerusalem as a monument to the triumph of the Lord over the grave. This day was celebrated throughout Christendom as the feast of the lifting-up of the Cross of Christ over all the world.

The hope that the time was at hand when all men would acknowledge the Lordship of the Saviour was premature. But this dream has never been forgotten. Christian people still work and pray for the time when all men everywhere will return to their Creator, the Crucified and Risen Lord. This is a day for rejoicing in that hope, as Abraham rejoiced in looking forward to Christ's coming, though he had only the most vague notion of what it would be like. We look forward with joyful anticipation to the day when all men shall find their Lord, and we work toward making him known in every corner of his creation.

O God, who by the passion of your blessed Son has made his shameful death to be unto us the sign of life and peace: Grant us so to glory in the Cross of Christ, that we may gladly suffer shame and loss.

Ninian

Apostle

Bishop in Galloway

Ninian was the son of a British chieftain and a Christian. He was educated in Rome and a personal friend of Martin of Tours. He resolved to convert the fierce tribes of southern Scotland to Christianity and eventually had some success in so doing.

Ninian established a monastery at Whithorn called "Candida Casa" (i.e. "White House"). The abbey church came to be called St. Martin's, after the friend of Ninian. The monastery at Whithorn became a center for missionary and charitable activities throughout that portion of southern Scotland commonly called Galloway.

Otherwise, we know practically nothing of Ninian. This is as much due to his success and popularity as to anything else, for the story of his life has been so glossed over and glorified by later admirers that it is impossible to separate fact from fancy. The student of history is confronted with a barrage of fascinating legends, some preposterous, some perhaps embellished truth, all praising the beloved apostle of Galloway.

O God, you have caused the light of gospel to shine in the land of Britain through your servant Ninian: Grant, we beseech you, that having his life and labours in remembrance, we may show forth our thankfulness unto you for the same by following the example of his zeal and patience; through Jesus Christ our Lord.

Henry Lay

Bishop of Easton

Minister of Reconciliation in the Civil War

Henry Lay was a native of Virginia and a priest in Alabama who, prior to the Civil War, boldly opposed both slavery and secession. On the eve of the War he was elected Missionary Bishop of the Southwest by the General Convention but was unable to assume those duties on account of the war.

During the Civil War he exercised a unique ministry to both Confederate and Union troops. He was once imprisoned by the invading forces, but ended up serving as their chaplain. He traveled widely throughout the war torn South, visiting hospitals and prisons and seeing to the care of all sorts of "homeless and neglected folk." His wartime ministry cost him his health, his home, and one child. He was present in Atlanta during the siege of that city and spent the evening prior to its destruction with General Sherman, interceding on behalf of the innocent and non-partisan victims of that campaign. His life and ministry was so clearly one that centered around the love of Christ and the service of mankind, that he retained the confidence of both sides in that traumatic war.

After the War he attended the General Convention and was largely responsible for effecting an immediate reunion of the Northern and Southern Episcopal Churches, thus sparing our church the long-standing division which characterized other religious groups of that time.

Theodore of Tarsus

Died September 19, 690

Archbishop of Canterbury

Organizer of the English Church

The 7th century was not an age of international under-standing and communication. However, the church clearly thought of itself as one world-wide body. In 668 an African monk recommended to Pope Vitalian of Rome that he dispatch Theodore, a Greek whose home-town was Tarsus (in modern Turkey), to England to fill the vacant See of Canterbury. And so it was done.

Theodore turned out to be one of the most brilliant and effective Archbishops England ever had. He visited all of England and secured the unity of the Christian people of the land under the leadership of Canterbury, generations before any leaders of state could accomplish such a thing. He called two important councils of the English Church, one at Hertford and one at Hatfield, which ratified the orthodoxy and unity of the Church of England. He was tolerant of local traditions as long as they did not generate heresy or schism.

Theodore was an exceptionally well-educated and cosmopolitan individual. He is said to have written much, but, unfortunately, his scholarly work was little appreciated in primitive England and none of it survives to this day. His monument is the Church of England: catholic, orthodox, and unified.

O God, raise up in your church good and faithful stew-ards of the mysteries of Christ, as you did in thy servant Theodore.

John Coleridge Patteson

Died September 20, 1871

Bishop of Melanesia

Missionary Martyrs of the South Seas

All the Christian world was shocked to learn of the murder of good Bishop Patteson by natives on the Island of Nukapu in the South Pacific.

Patteson had been among the flowers of England's youth. He was educated at Eton and at Oxford University. He had rejected a promising and comfortable career in England and had given himself utterly to the task of civilizing and Christianizing the native peoples of Polynesia and Melanesia. For nearly twenty years he had served patiently and unselfishly, founding schools, hospitals, and churches, teaching, preaching and giving the sacraments to the natives of those lands. He also sought out and ministered to British settlers in those areas. He once presented the entire population of Pitcairn Island for confirmation, following the reconciliation of the *Bounty* mutineers with the British Government.

He was seriously concerned about the wanton practice of "blackbirding," or slave raiding which went on in the islands and was working vigorously to stop it. Nukapu had recently been victimized by such raiders and it was for this reason that Patteson's missionary ship, "The Southern Cross," anchored off that Island on this day in 1871 and the Bishop went ashore. He was killed that night by some of those whom he was trying to serve.

Matthew
Evangelist

Apostle of the Lord

Matthew, sometimes called Levi, was a tax collector and, as any student of history or scripture knows, that put him in a wicked and despised class in 1st century Palestine. In fact, he was sitting in his tax office when Jesus called him to be a disciple. As if it were not scandalous enough for Jesus to include such a person in his group, he allowed and encouraged Matthew to bring in more tax collectors. Of course, Jesus demanded and got such a radical change in these men that they were no longer recognizable as tax collectors.

The Apostle Matthew is not generally regarded as the author of the gospel which bears his name, but he probably contributed the essential information which went into its writing.

We have a lot of conflicting legends about his later life, but no reliable information.

We thank you, heavenly Father, for the witness of your apostle and evangelist Matthew to the gospel of your Son our Saviour; and we pray that, after his example, we may with ready wills and hearts obey the calling of our Lord to follow him; through Jesus Christ our Lord, who lives and reigns with you and the Holy Spirit, one God, now and ever.

Sergius

Abbot of Holy Trinity, Moscow

Hero of Christian Russia

In Sergius' youth the Christians of Russia were suffering under the "Tartar Yoke," dominated and oppressed by pagan invaders. The Christian community was weak, divided, and confused. Under the vigorous leadership of Sergius and the monks of Holy Trinity monastery, they gained new hope. Sergius is best remembered as the beloved abbot who inspired Dmitri, Prince of Moscow, to resist Tartar domination. Equally important were his efforts to reform and revive the Russian Orthodox monasteries. He personally supervised the founding of over forty new monasteries.

Sergius is usually associated with the armed resistance to the Tartars, but he was also a great peace maker. He was often successful in mediating disputes among princes and on four occasions he averted civil war. Sergius was a man of deep faith and strong character. He was peasant born, hearty, neighborly, and practical. He struggled to keep the communal spirit alive among his monks and among the Christian people of Russia. He taught, by word and deed, absolute devotion to Christ as known in the Holy Eucharist and unselfish service to others.

Almighty and everlasting God, we give you thanks for the purity and strength with which you did endow your servant Sergius; and we pray that by your grace we may have a like power to hallow and confirm our souls.

Lancelot Andrewes

Died September 26, 1626

Bishop of Winchester

Scholar, Preacher, Pastor of 17th Century England

One of the brightest lights of 17th century England was Lancelot Andrewes, beloved pastor to the court of King James I and as fine a preacher as ever mounted the pulpit of St. Paul's, London. Andrewes, a Cambridge graduate, was a tireless and accurate scholar, the master of some fifteen languages. Perhaps the best Hebraist of his day, he was chiefly responsible for translating the Old Testament of the King James Version of the Bible.

As a young clergyman, his eloquent and erudite preaching attracted the attention of Queen Elizabeth, who offered him the great bishopric of Salisbury and later of Ely. He declined both, but accepted the position of Dean of Westminster. Finally, his well loved friend, King James I, persuaded him to take episcopal orders. He is best remembered as the saintly Bishop of Winchester.

He had profound insight into human nature and compassion for human weakness. He was a versatile and liberal pastor and had little use for the harshness and austerity of Calvinism, so popular in the British Isles in his day.

Lancelot Andrewes' lengthy sermons are far too academic for modern ears, but his book, *Private Devotions,* still enjoys perennial popularity.

Help us to follow the good examples of your servant Lancelot, and of all those who loved and served you.

Saint Michael and All Angels September 29

The Powerful and Elusive Messengers of God

The scriptural word *angel* (Greek: *angelos*) means, literally, a messenger. These messengers from God can be visible or invisible, and may assume human or non-human forms. Christians have always felt themselves to be tended by healthful spirits; swift, powerful, enlightening, and sometimes highly personable. These kindly spirits are often depicted in Christian art in human form, with wings to signify their swiftness and spacelessness, with swords to signify their power, and with dazzling raiment to signify their ability to enlighten. Unfortunately, this type of representation has led many to dismiss the angels as "just another mythical beast, like the unicorn, the griffin, or the sphinx."

Of the many angels spoken of in the Bible, only four are called by name: Michael, Gabriel, Uriel, and Raphael. The Archangel Michael is the powerful agent of God who wards off evil from God's people and delivers peace to them at the end of this life's mortal struggle. "Michaelmas," as his feast is called in England, has long been one of the popular celebrations of the Christian Year in many parts of the world. Michael has been the patron of countless churches, including Mont-Saint-Michel, the monastry-fortress off the coast of Normandy that figured so prominently in medieval English history, and Coventry Cathedral, England's most famous modern church building.

We thank you, Lord, for your continuing help.

Jerome

Died September 30, 420

Priest and Monk of Bethlehem

Theologian and Translator of Scripture

Jerome is chiefly remembered as the translator of the most famous and widely used version of the Bible ever published, the Latin Vulgate. In the 5th century most people in Western Europe spoke Latin, yet there was not an accurate or complete Latin text of the Bible. Jerome translated the entire Bible into Latin from its original Hebrew and Greek. He translated the sacred text into the common "street language" of his day, called "vulgar" Latin. In time this work came to be regarded as a "classic," but when it was published it was the subject of considerable controversy. Jerome deliberately did not use the elevated "Ciceronian" Latin with which he was so familiar, because he was warned in a dream that he was becoming a "Ciceronian and not a Christian."

A native of Strido, Italy, Jerome traveled widely and was educated in Rome, Antioch, Jerusalem, and Alexandria. He got envolved in practically every important issue of his day and was one of the most vehement adversaries of the Arian and Pelagian heresies. His correspondence reflects a strong faith and a sound mind as well as a passion for truth and integrity. He settled finally in Bethlehem as the head of a monastic community. One of history's greatest scholars and translators became a great pastor. "Now," he said, "we have to translate the words of scripture into deeds!"

Remigius

Bishop of Rheims

Apostle of the Franks

We know very little of Remigius (sometimes "Remi"). He lived in an age of relative obscurity. However, two startling events punctuate his biography and have assured his lasting fame.

First, he was consecrated Bishop of Rheims at age 22. In some times and places the consecration of one so young might be simply a reflection of the decadent politics of the church. In Remigius' case he seems to have been elected because of the genuine esteem in which he was held.

Second, he converted and baptised Clovis, the first Christian King of France. Remigius was a tireless missionary among the pagan Franks, and this event, which probably took place in 496, was the crowning achievement of his life.

Remigius was credited with a number of miracles and was perhaps the greatest preacher of France in his day. Through Remigius the light of the gospel shone forth in a dark and savage land and a new age and civilization was born: Christian France.

O God, the light of the faithful and shepherd of souls, who did call your servant Remigius to feed your sheep by his word, and guide them by his example: Grant us, we pray you, to keep the faith which he taught, and to follow in his footsteps; through Jesus Christ our Lord.

Francis of Assisi

Friar

Brother of the Poor

One of the boldest and most spirited figures in history, it is a shame that Francis is sometimes dimissed as simply a quiet "bird-watcher." Actually he was an outspoken and controversial "social activist." He was one of the greatest preachers of all time. His concern with poverty and ecology give him a strikingly modern quality. Although he was a wealthy cloth merchant's son, he gave all he had to help the poor and was contented with only the barest necessities for himself. He vigorously opposed the abuse of political power, particularly when it was wielded by the Bishop of Rome.

Francis was effective in initiating sweeping social and economic reforms. He was a popular singer, often called "God's Troubadour." His most famous hymn, "Canticle to Brother Sun" (307 in *The Hymnal 1940*), has stood the test of time. Francis founded one of the strongest and most dynamic religious orders in Christendom. Today we find Franciscan Friars in both the Roman and Anglican communions.

Most high, almighty, and good Lord: Grant your people grace to renounce gladly the vanities of this world, that, after the example of blessed Francis, we may for love of you delight in all your creatures, with perfectness of joy; through Jesus Christ our Lord.

William Tyndale

Died October 6, 1536

Priest

Scholar and Translator of the Bible

Change, even the most innocent and constructive, comes hard to men and societies. When William Tyndale, a careful and competent scholar and priest, prepared a translation of the Bible into English, he suddenly found himself treated as a scoundrel and a radical, even by those from whom he had expected the most support, the intellectuals and churchmen of England.

At Oxford, as a student, and at Cambridge, as a teacher, he had found great truth and guidance for his life from the scriptures, which were then available only to those who could read Latin, or in the partial and sometimes inaccurate version of John Wyclif. Tyndale wanted to make the Bible available to Englishmen in their native tongue. When his bishop got word of the project, he chastised Tyndale for such "revolutionary" activity and eventually made things so uncomfortable for the scholar that he had to leave England and flee to Germany, where the first edition of the Tyndale Version of the Bible was published.

In spite of Tyndale's piety, scholarship, and good intentions, his work brought nothing but wrath from the English authorities. He was captured, tried as a heretic and schismatic, strangled, and publicly burned at Vilvorde, Belgium, in 1536.

We thank you, Lord, for the constancy and zeal of your servant William.

Robert Grosseteste

Bishop of Lincoln

Died October 9, 1253

Great Pastor, Reformer, and Scholar

Had the leaders of the 13th century paid more attention to this wise and devout pastor and scholar, many of the disasters of the next three centuries might have been avoided. Robert was a very bright peasant lad from Suffolk, England, who was educated by the church at Oxford and Paris. His charm, intellect, and piety gained the attention of the authorities and he was made Rector of Oxford and eventually consecrated Bishop of Lincoln. In that position his chief concern was for the welfare of his flock, both spiritually and temporally. He visited all the churches in the diocese and quickly relieved many of the prominent clergy because they were neglecting their pastoral duties. He staunchly opposed the corrupt practice of the Bishop of Rome of making Italian priests absentee clergy for English churches. He insisted that his priests spend their time in the service of their people, in prayer, and in study. He went on a pilgrimage to Rome where he spoke out boldly against many of the corruptions of the church. His sermons were moving and prophetic, but they went unheeded by the Papacy.

Back in England, where he was welcomed as a hero, he witnessed the signing of the Magna Carta, which he firmly supported, and continued his inexhaustable quest for knowledge, writing, studying and teaching astronomy, philosophy, optics, physics, poetry, and Holy Scripture. Grosseteste was a man of piety, integrity, courage, and compassion.

Samuel Isaac Joseph Schereschewsky

Died October 15, 1906

Bishop of Shanghai

Apostle to the Chinese

It is hard to imagine a more cosmopolitan and ecumenical character than Samuel Schereschewsky, a Lithuanian Jew, trained in a Rabbinic school in Poland, an imigrant to America, baptised by a Baptist minister and educated in Presbyterian and Episcopalian seminaries. He went to China as a missionary in the service of the Episcopal Church and was eventually consecrated Bishop of Shanghai.

He was a robust and active man whose life style was severely disrupted when he suffered from a stroke which incapacitated him and forced his return to America. For the rest of his life he was confined to a wheelchair. Undaunted, it was in this condition that he did his most famous work. Always an excellent linguist, he now gave his full attention to the translation of the entire Bible into two chinese dialects. Eventually it was necessary for him to return to China where Chinese scribes could complete the details of this monumental work. Leaving China for the last time, he was taken to Japan where the American Bible Society was publishing his work and there he died. The trip had, presumably, been too much for his old and exhausted frame. The Lord had given vast and inscrutable China an apostle worthy of her nature and dignity.

Hugh Latimer and Nicholas Ridley

Died October 16, 1555

Bishops

Reformers and Martyrs

"Today we shall light such a fire in England as shall never be extinguished." With these words Latimer and Ridley went to the stake and were burned to death on this day in 1555 at Oxford.

Besides being burned together, Latimer and Ridley had much in common. Both were English Bishops with strong Protestant sympathies. Each was an exceptionally fine preacher in an age of great preachers. Both were Cambridge men. Both were social reformers.

Latimer was the sometime Bishop of Worcester, who first rose to prominence in the days of Thomas Cardinal Wolsey and Henry VIII. In those days he was one of only twelve priests licensed to preach anywhere in England. He first gained a reputation as a social reformer and then as a church reformer. This alone was enough to put Queen Mary on his heels.

Nicholas Ridley, the sometime Bishop of London, was equally infamous to Mary's "bloody" inquisitors. During his brief episcopate he had seen to the founding of three hospitals and had contributed significantly to the new *Book of Common Prayer*. His "Protestantizing" sermons brought down upon his head the wrath of Mary's most unreconciliatory regime.

Yet Latimer and Ridley had, indeed, lit a fire in England that was not to be extingushed.

Ignatius

Died October 17, c.115

Bishop of Antioch

Bishop and Martyr

When the Roman Emperor, Trajan, ordered that Ignatius, Bishop of Antioch, be brought to Rome for public execution as an "atheist and subversive," he made a serious blunder. The journey which Ignatius was compelled to take was long and calls were made at numerous ports. Few men were unimpressed by the sight of the saintly old bishop being hauled in chains to his death. Crowds of Christians and Christian sympathizers gathered at his ports of call to cheer him on. Others joined him and helped record and distribute his letters which soon became famous. In these letters Ignatius rejoiced at his opportunity to witness for Christ through martyrdom. He warned Christians against the grave danger of heresy within their ranks and urged them to follow the teaching and practice of their duly elected and consecrated bishops. He was one of the first important literary defenders of the three-fold ministry: bishops, priests, and deacons.

Ignatius' letters to the Christians in Ephesus, Magnesia, Trolles, Rome, Philadelphia, and Smyrna, are among our most valuable documents of the early church. He was brutally put to death before a mob in the Colosseum at Rome, but the testimony of his life and letters lived on to inspire his fellows in Christ.

We thank you for your servant Ignatius who triumphed over suffering and despised death.

123

Luke the Evangelist

Early Christian Physician and Historian

Luke was a Gentile and a physician. He was probably a slave, since most physicians were in those days. He was a Christian convert and a frequent companion of Paul. He probably ministered medically to Paul. In Christian literature he is most often referred to as "The Beloved Physician."

Luke exhibited a sense of history, unique among the Evangelists. He was not an eyewitness to the events of Jesus' life but tried to present an accurate and orderly account of those events which he had heard about from his sources. His writings, Luke and Acts in the New Testament, give us an historical narrative which remains altogether appealing, even to modern ears. Luke has given us the familiar Christmas story and the parable of the Good Samaritan which the other evangelists neglect.

According to tradition, Luke lived to a ripe old age. Unlike so many of the leaders of the early church, he seems to have died of natural causes and quite peacefully.

Almighty God, who inspired your servant Saint Luke, the physician, to set forth in the gospel the love and healing power of your Son: Graciously continue in your Church the like love and power to heal, to the praise and glory of your Name; through Jesus Christ our Lord, who lives and reigns with you in the unity of the Holy Spirit, one God, now and forever.

Henry Martyn

Died October 19, 1812

Priest

Missionary to India and Persia

One good example is worth a thousand exhortations. The good example of young Henry Martyn lead to a flurry of enthusiasm for the Church of England's missionary efforts in India and the East.

Martyn was born in Truro, England, and educated at Cambridge, where he was a friend of Chaplain Simeon. Henry was a very bright, lovable, and dedicated young man, and it was probably Simeon who encouraged him to take up a missionary vocation. In 1805 Martyn became a chaplain for the East India Company, upon Simeon's recommendation, and sailed to India. There he served the Church in Calcutta, founded schools at Patna and Cawnpore, and translated the New Testament and the Book of Common Prayer into Hindustani. He traveled widely, preaching, teaching, and helping those in need in every way he could.

He went to Persia and there translated the New Testament into Persian. Travel in those days brought few pleasures and many hazards. Exhausted and seeking some respite for soul and body he went into Asia Minor where the climate and civilization were somewhat more hospitable. There, at Tokat (in modern Turkey), he became very ill and was befriended by Armenian Christians. He died there at age 31 and buried by Armenian clergy.

We thank you, Lord, for Henry and all missionaries.

James of Jerusalem

Died October 23, c.62

Brother of Jesus, Apostle and Martyr

James was, according to the Gospels of Matthew and Mark, and according to Paul, a brother of Jesus. Yet, he was not a believer during the Lord's earthly ministry. Jesus appeared to him after the resurrection and he was converted.

He soon rose to prominence in the church and became the Bishop of Jerusalem. He presided over the important Council in Jerusalem which decided to permit Gentiles to join the church. As the church grew and prospered, he became less and less popular with the authorities. According to the highly reliable historian, Josephus, he was eventually stoned and clubbed to death by a mob.

James of Jerusalem is usually considered to be the author of the Epistle of James. If this is the case, he certainly had a clear insight into the Lord's message and ministry and its relationship to the Old Covenant.

Grant, we pray, O God, that after the example of your servant James, the brother of our Lord, your Church may give itself continually to prayer, and to the reconciliation of all who are at variance and enmity; through Jesus Christ our Lord, who lives and reigns with you in the unity of the Holy Spirit, one God, now and for ever.

Note: *Forward Day by Day* is a manual of daily Bible readings and devotions, issued quarterly.

Alfred the Great

Died October 26, 899

King of Wessex

A Christian Prince in a Savage Land

In the "Dark Ages," when much of Britain was yet un-Christianized and uncivilized, there arose among the West Saxons in Southern England a great king, who was an example of piety and learning. Alfred the Great was wise and courageous and used his temporal power for the spiritual, intellectual, and economic advancement of his people.

In his youth, Alfred knew the terror of mortal illness, of invasion, and of the death of loved ones. In the savage warfare of his day he was brave, strong, and cunning. He was not a man unacquainted with grief and hardship or unfamiliar with the harsh realities of life. From the monks of Wessex and from his teachers in Rome, he learned a kinder, gentler, nobler way of life than most of his people had even been exposed to, although they were at least nominally Christian. When, in his maturity, he became the most powerful of the Anglo-Saxon Kings, he administered justice with insight and fairness, laying the foundation for much of the best in English law. He founded a palace school which was unequaled in Northern Europe.

He is well remembered in stone at his capital city, Winchester, and well commemorated in modern leaders who truly seek the moral, physical, and intellectual betterment of their people. King Alfred the Great was in fact what King Arthur was to become in fancy; the model Christian King.

Simon and Jude

Apostles

Christian tradition has long associated these two apostles with one another. They may have traveled and worked together. Historically speaking, we know very little about Jude and less about Simon.

Jude, in modern times, has enjoyed a marvelous reputation as a patron of lost or desperate causes. He was, presumably, the author of the New Testament Epistle which bears his name. In that case he was a man with some skill in verbal expression. His happy phrase, "contend for the faith, once for all delivered to the saints," is one which has certainly endured and been much quoted. The last two verses of that Epistle are an unforgettable doxology.

Simon is called a "Zealot" in Holy Scripture, but it is difficult to determine just what that meant. There were many Zealot groups in Jewish history, most of them obscure, and they were not all alike by any means.

A strong and old Eastern tradition holds that Simon and Jude were apostles to Persia. If this is true it explains, to some extent, our lack of historical information on them and also why they are usually put together.

O God, we thank you for the glorious company of the apostles, and especially on this day for Saint Simon and Saint Jude; and we pray that, as they were faithful and zealous in their mission, so we may with ardent devotion make known among the nations the love and mercy of our Lord and Savior Jesus Christ.

James Hannington

Died October 29, 1885

Bishop of Eastern Equatorial Africa

Missionary and Martyr

James Hannington was one of those Englishmen who caught a vision of what needed to be done on "the Dark Continent" and set out to offer all he could in service for Africa's people. He served for a time as a missionary priest in Eastern Africa, but had to return to England because of ill health. In 1884 he went back to Africa, having recovered, carrying with him episcopal orders. He was enthroned at Mombasa and set out to establish a series of mission stations west to Lake Victoria Nyanza by way of Mount Kilimanjaro. A new king had just ascended the throne in Uganda and when he heard of Bishop Hannington's approach he feared it was an attack on his kingdom and dispatched warriors to eliminate the problem. Hannington and his companions soon found themselves surrounded by hostile warriors. A group of them encircled the bishop and paused before plunging their spears into him just long enough for him to say his last words, "Go tell your king that I die for the people of Buganda, and that I have purchased the road to Uganda with my life." Within the next few days many of the native Christians of the area were brutally tortured and martyred.

But the story did not end there. The church prevailed and today thrives among the natives of Uganda, Rwanda, and Burundi.

Bless all who serve in the land of Africa as witnesses.

The Champions of Christ

Our English word "saint," derived from the Latin *sanctus,* is used in a variety of ways. Literally it means "holy," "set apart for God," "consecrated," or "dedicated." In the New Testament *hagios,* the Greek word for "saint," is used to refer to all church members, many of whom were far from exemplary Christians. Paul sometimes scolded the "saints" for their corrupt and decadent ways.

When we use the word "saint" in the context of All Saints Day we refer to those Christians who have lived such hallowed lives, yielding so fully to the Holy Spirit, showing such love for God and his human creatures, that their examples are treasured and emulated. These individuals, a few of whom are remembered in this little book, are the champions of Christ and his church, and the heroes of the faithful.

In medieval times the Roman Catholic Church developed an elaborate system for designating and selecting the saints, called "canonization." The Eastern Orthodox and Anglican Churches have been much less systematic in deciding who would be called a saint. Virtually all Christians acknowledge that it is ultimately God who decides who his "holy ones" are and none of our judgments or acclamations presume to make such decisions for him. Our intention is rather to share and rejoice in the knowledge of those who have done good things in his Name in all times and places.

Commemoration of All Faithful Departed

A Cloud of Witnesses

If we have trouble thinking of dear old Aunt Polly or Uncle John as being "saints," now is the appropriate time to formally remember them. There are countless departed souls who were faithful Christians but who could hardly be regarded as exemplary "saints." We like to remember them and to give thanks to God publicly for them.

This occasion, sometimes called "All Souls Day," is a twin feast of "All Saints Day." It has been observed in the Eastern Church from very early times and was introduced into Western Europe in the 10th century. The 16th century English Reformers cut this festival out of the Church Year because they did not like to distinguish between "all saints" and "all souls." The New Testament makes no such distinction but, rather, refers to all Christians as saints, stressing the fact that salvation is a gift from God and that none of us earns a special place in his kingdom by our good deeds. This is a good time to remember the unspectacular children of God; those whose Christian witness may have been weak or faltering, but who are still very dear and important to God and to us.

O God, who has brought us near to an innumerable company of Angels, and to the spirits of just men made perfect: Grant us during our pilgrimage to abide in their fellowship, and to become partakers of their joy.

Richard Hooker

Died November 3, 1600

Priest

Anglican Theologian

The master theologian of the English Reformation, Richard Hooker, was a relatively obscure person in his own day. His famous tome, *The Laws of Ecclesiastical Polity,* was a landmark in English literature, philosophy, and churchmanship. There has never been a more thorough and convincing apologist for Anglicanism, yet we know little of his life. He was an Oxford graduate and served several relatively undistinguished parishes during his somewhat short ministry (he seems to have died at age 46).

Some of his basic positions and arguments are so familiar to modern Episcopalians as to seem almost like cliches. He argued for the reasonable and reverent use of Holy Scripture, rejecting the Roman Catholic disregard for scripture and the Puritan's literal and mechanical view of it. He saw the church as a living organism, rather like a family, and not as a static and impersonal institution that could never change, nor as a purely "spiritual" and intellectual association of subscribers.

It would certainly do violence to Hooker's own teaching if modern Episcopalians regarded him as the definitive teacher and final authority. But one can say that Richard Hooker best expressed, intellectually, the mind and spirit of 17th century Anglicanism.

Enrich us by the teaching of your servant Richard.

Willibrord

Died November 7, 738

Archbishop of Utrecht

Apostle to Holland

Willibrord is one of the most celebrated of the Anglo-Saxon saints of the early Middle Ages. He was highly praised by both the Venerable Bede and Alcuin of York, the major historians of that period. He was a native of Northumbria, England, and a student of Wilfred, famous Bishop of Northumbria. He was ordained a priest in Ireland where he studied under some the best Christian teachers of Britain.

After an arduous, but successful, pilgrimage to Rome, Willibrord set out, with the blessing of the Bishop of Rome, to convert the fierce and pagan Frisians of what is today called the Netherlands or Holland. The details of that venture are not accurately recorded. We only know that it was highly successful. Willibrord established a strong and dedicated Christian "beachhead" at Utrecht, where he eventually became Archbishop.

Willibrord typifies a long standing relationship between English and Dutch Christians. Today the historic Diocese of Utrecht is in full communion with the Church of England.

O almighty God, who in your providence did choose your servant Willibrord to be an apostle to the Frisian people, to bring those who were wandering in darkness and error to the true light and knowledge of you: Grant us so to walk in that light, that we may come at last to the light of everlasting life.

Leo the Great

Died November 10, 461

Bishop of Rome

Bishop and Statesman in the Dark Ages

Leo, Bishop of Rome, captured the imagination of generations of Europeans when he stood before the terrible horde of the Huns and persuaded them to withdraw to the Danube. He settled the most heated and dangerous theological dispute since Nicaea, when his legates ended the Eutychian controversy. He succeeded in getting imperial and ecclesiastical endorsement for his claim that the Bishop of Rome was primate of the Catholic Church in Western Europe. Leo the Great was a statesman par excellence and is sometimes called the "Founder of the Papacy." He appeared in a very troubled time in the "Dark Ages" of Western Europe and was a veritable saviour not only of the church but of law and order of any kind, indeed, of civilization.

Leo's most famous written work, his *Tome,* remains a classic statement of Christian doctrine. His sermons and letters still reveal to us a clear, forcible, and intelligent pastor, though not an unusually brilliant or profound one.

Almighty, everlasting God, whose servant Leo steadfastly confessed the true faith of your Son our Saviour Jesus Christ to be Very God and Very Man: Grant that we may hold fast to this faith, and evermore magnify his holy Name; through the same your Son Jesus Christ our Lord, who lives and reigns with you and the Holy Spirit ever, one God, world without end.

Martin

Bishop of Tours

A Patron of Soldiers and of Justice

Martin was reared a pagan and became an officer in the Roman army. As a young officer serving in the Province of Gaul (France) he became an "inquirer" or catechumen of the Christian faith. At Amiens he encountered a beggar who was cold and naked. Moved with compassion he ripped his own officer's cloak in two and gave the beggar half. From that time on he resolved to become a Christian and follow the Lord's way of life.

After obtaining a discharge from the army, he traveled about a good deal but finally settled at Poitiers where he and Hilary, the Bishop of Poitiers, founded a religious community. Martin was eventually elected Bishop of Tours and in that capacity he became famous as a pastor and evangelist. He succeeded in establishing parishes and monasteries throughout the region. Martin was a strong advocate of justice in a time and place when power seemed to rule. He was indignant and protested any mistreatment of heretics or pagans by Christians, and vice versa.

Martin became a patron saint of France. He was also very popular among the old Celtic Christians of Britain. Augustine, the first Archbishop of Canterbury, was startled upon arriving at what he presumed to be pagan Britain, to find a Christian Church, St. Martin's, at Canterbury.

O Lord, may we, too, withstand the world's temptations.

Charles Simeon

Priest

Died November 12, 1836

Chaplain to Cambridge

Frequently, when a person has an overpowering and deeply personal religious experience he will turn away from the relatively cold, static, and worldly "institutional" church. This need not and should not be the case. Charles Simeon is a beautiful example of an evangelical Christian whose life was changed by a personal religious experience while an undergraduate, but who remained all his life a most loyal churchman. He always saw the church as his proper home and as a real vehicle of grace for all men. He was one of the foremost evangelical preachers of his day, yet remained, also, a staunch advocate of the *Book of Common Prayer* and of bishops. Although his position was reasonable, sound, and just, it exposed him to severe criticism from both the "High Church" and the "Evangelical" parties. He was ridiculed, insulted, and threatened with physical violence by one group and then by the other.

Charles Simeon spent his entire ministry as a chaplain at Cambridge University. There his academic ability, his talent as a preacher, and his genuine concern for people enabled him to exert a great influence for good on a generation of Cambridge men. He was an excellent student of the Bible and led many young men to discover the sacred book's relevance and message for their lives. He was one of the founders of the Church Missionary Society.

Samuel Seabury *Consecrated November 14, 1784*

Bishop of Connecticut

First American Bishop

On this day in 1784 the first American bishop was consecrated in Aberdeen, Scotland, in a quiet ceremony in the private chapel of Bishop John Skinner. In this way the episcopate was brought to America and it was possible for Americans to organize an episcopal church, independent of the Church of England. The English bishops could not legally consecrate an American bishop who would not swear allegiance to the English Crown and for this reason Seabury had to go to Scotland for episcopal orders. Soon the English laws were modified to allow for the consecration of American bishops in the English succession.

Samuel Seabury of Connecticut was a controversial figure and hardly conformed to the traditional idea of a "saint." Unlike our other early bishops, White of Pennsylvania, Provoost of New York, and Madison of Virginia, Seabury opposed the American Revolution. For this, and because he was considered terribly "high church" for the times, he was not generally popular. Yet he performed an invaluable service for the American Church in securing the episcopacy for her. Feelings ran high against bishops in those days, especially in New England. It took considerable courage and determination for him to go to England and Scotland and then return to Connecticut as a bishop.

Grant that we may serve you diligently in our day.

Margaret

Died November 16, 1093

Queen of Scotland

Exemplary Wife, Queen, and Mother

When the Normans successfully invaded England in 1066 the Anglo-Saxon royalty fled from England. Margaret, a cousin of the defeated king, fled with her mother and sister to Scotland where they found refuge in the court of the Scottish King Malcolm. Margaret soon married King Malcolm and became Scotland's most beloved and revered queen.

She was always a deeply religious person, showing great interest in the church and great compassion for the poor. In her youth she considered a religious vocation and in her maturity she found one, as wife and mother. Her firm and loving influence on the king, the church, her children, and the people, virtually renewed the life of the whole nation of Scotland. Under her influence monasteries, schools, orphanages, and hospitals were founded and the quality of life greatly improved in the land. One tragic aspect of Scottish life about which Margaret could not nothing was that of clan warfare and blood feuds. Malcolm was treacherously slain at Alnwick in 1093 and the grief-stricken Margaret died a few days later. Their son, David, became one of Scotland's finest kings. Their daughter, Matilda, married the English King Henry I and so Margaret and Malcolm are ancestors of the present British Royal Family.

As you did endue with zeal and charity your servant Margaret, so endue us.

138

Hugh

Bishop of Lincoln

A Bold and Beloved English Bishop

Hugh was as thoroughly attractive and virile a figure as ever graced the pages of English history. He was an able sportsman, a lover of children and of animals, an excellent administrator, and a man whose humor and kindness literally charmed the socks off the English court. Although a man of strong temper himself, Hugh was one of the very few who could calm the raging of King Henry II.

Hugh was a native of Avalon, Burgundy, in what is now France. He came to England as abbot of the Charterhouse monastery at Witham in Somerset. Later he was elected Bishop of Lincoln, then the largest diocese in England.

He was a vigorous opponent of injustice of any kind, a sort of ecclesiastical Robin Hood. He boldly supported the peasants in defiance of the king's harsh forest laws. On more than one occasion he faced, alone, rioting mobs, incensed against the Jews. He refused to allow the powerful and popular King Richard I to raid the church's treasury to support his crusades. If ever the title "prince of the church" was appropriate for a bishop, it was appropriate for Hugh of Lincoln.

O God, as your servant Hugh did feed your sheep by his word, and guide them by his example, so may we.

Hilda

Died November 18, 680

Abbess of Whitby

Grand Lady of the British Church

The lovely Hilda was like a breath of Spring in the dark winter of 7th century England. She was born of the pagan royalty of Northumbria. When she was thirteen years old her great uncle, King Edwin, was converted and she was baptised with his household. She was a lady of some rank and station and, although deeply touched by the new faith, hesitated to enter upon a religious vocation until she was over thirty. Eventually she founded a monastery herself at Whitby, with the help of Aidan, Bishop of Lindisfarne. The Whitby monastery was mixed, men and women, and became a great center of the old British Church. There, according to Bede, Hilda oversaw the careful teaching of Holy Scripture, "by word and example, righteousness and mercy and purity, and especially peace and charity." There the famous Anglo-Saxon poet, Caedmon, was befriended and there he composed much of his work. There in 664 King Oswy called the church council which decided on the Romanization of the old British (Celtic) Church. Hilda was not pleased with this decision which seriously changed the worship and discipline of her community. However, she gracefully accepted it, relinquishing local customs in the interest of the unity and order of the Universal Church.

O Lord, may we have a like power to hallow and conform our souls and bodies to your holy will.

Elizabeth

Princess of Hungary

Sister of the Unfortunate

Being born "with a silver spoon in one's mouth" does not assure security in life, and one's own generosity to others does not guarantee repayment in kind by others. Elizabeth was well born, the daughter of the King of Hungary, carefully reared and wisely married to the noble Landgrave of Thuringia, Germany. She was a loving and exemplary wife and mother. However, when she was only twenty years old, her husband was killed and she and her children became the wards of her husband's cruel and selfish brother, Henry Raspe. Eventually he expelled Elizabeth and her little ones from the family home, Wartburg Castle, and this in the dead of winter.

Elizabeth sought refuge in the church in Marburg, but even there she was not kindly treated. The stern, powerful, and insensitive priest, Conrad, called "the Master of Marburg," had her children taken from her and placed her in a convent of women Franciscans, "Poor Clares." There she was treated with almost sadistic severity. "Like grass beaten by a thunderstorm," to use her own phrase, she revived to become the most beloved "sister of the poor" of Marburg. She often sewed garments for poor children until her fingers bled, or went days without sleep caring for the sick. She met an early death and even old Conrad repented and acknowledged that he had, indeed, mistreated a saint.

Clement

Bishop of Rome

Pastor and Epistler of the Early Church

Clement was, as best we can determine, the third Bishop of Rome. He is believed to be the Clement mentioned in *Philippians 4:3* and he may well have known Paul and Peter personally. He was in all probability an ex-slave of the family of Titus Flavius Clemens, relatives of the Emperor Domitian. However, his fame rests primarily on a letter he wrote to the Christians in Corinth in about 95. It is usually called I Clement and has often been regarded as canonical scripture.

This beautiful epistle is an admonition to the Corinthian Christians to be patient with one another, to obey the legitimate church authorities and to concentrate on demonstrating to each other and to the world the wonderful love of Christ. "Let each man be subject to his neighbor," wrote Clement. "Let the strong care for the weak, and let the weak respect the strong. Let the rich provide for the poor, and let the poor give thanks that God has given him one to supply his need. Let the wise man show his wisdom, not in words, but in good deeds."

Clement's verses on love are second only to those of Paul himself. Also, like Paul, he builds a strong case for obedience to church leadership and admonishes against rebellious spirits, envy, jealousy, and strife.

O God, raise up faithful witnesses today, like Clement, who will set forth the truth of your salvation.

Andrew

Apostle of the Lord

Andrew was the brother of Simon Peter. In fact, he was in part responsible for Peter's call, for he went and "found his brother Simon . . . and brought him to Jesus." Andrew was a fisherman by trade. He was a follower of John the Baptist before being called by Jesus as a disciple.

It was Andrew who told Jesus about the boy with loaves and fishes at the feeding of the five thousand. Andrew also assisted in the distribution of the food on that occasion.

Tradition tells us that Andrew worked among the Scythians, ancient inhabitants of a part of modern Russia. He has long been the patron saint of Russia. Andrew is also the patron saint of Scotland, and the Scottish flag bears the X shaped cross usually associated with him. It is believed that he was bound to such a cross and thus met his death at the hands of angry pagans. Today members of the Brotherhood of St. Andrew emulate his action of going to find his brother and taking him to Christ. The Brotherhood of St. Andrew is an informal association of men and boys in the Episcopal Church in the U.S.A.

Almighty God, who gave such grace to your apostle Andrew, that he readily obeyed the calling of your son Jesus Christ, and followed him without delay: Grant, we pray, that we, who are called by your holy Word, may offer ourselves in glad obedience to your service.

Nicholas Ferrar

Died December 1, 1637

Deacon

Founder of Little Gidding

Every generation of Christians seems to produce its own kind of religious community, from ancient Athos to modern Taize. Little Gidding in Huntingtonshire, England, was one of its generations most famous religious communities. Nicholas Ferrar was the founder and chaplain of Little Gidding.

He was well-born, well-educated, and well-traveled. Ferrar was a Member of Parliament and a trustee of the Virginia Company. When he was thirty-four years old he retired to his family estate at Little Gidding and, with a number of friends, organized a semi-monastic community of men and women. Members of the community followed a very strict rule of life, using the *Book of Common Prayer* for their guide. They did not take vows of celibacy and did not withdraw from the world. They were very active in providing for the poor, operating a free school and a hospital. Through three decades Little Gidding established and maintained an impeccable reputation for charity and godly living. However, the Puritans, at the height of their raging against the prayerbook and "popery," broke up the community, violently. They contemptuously called it a "protestant nunnery." When the Puritan tide ebbed and the church was restored in England, Little Gidding was not revived. However, its spirit of real Christian community and of service to human beings in need, is continually being renewed in the church.

Channning Moore Williams

Died December 2, 1910

Bishop of Japan

Missionary to the Chinese and Japanese

This quiet, shy, patient, and scholarly priest first entered Japan as a missionary in 1859 after several years experience in China. He was greeted as an "evil corrupter" and a "foreign devil." His only colleague, John Liggins, was severely beaten by a mob and had to return to America. Williams carried on in his inimitable way, and gradually gained the confidence of the Japanese.

He lived in stark simplicity, adopted a distinctly Japanese life style, and became a master of the Japanese language. Williams was a native of Virginia and the American Civil War brought great personal grief to him as well as a dearth of missionary funds. When peace came, he toured America, raising money for his work, was consecrated Bishop and returned to Japan. Gradually the Lord's work prospered.

St. Paul's University (Kyoto), St. Luke's Hospital (Tokyo), and numerous lesser institutions were started. Perhaps the greatest joy in William's life came with the organization of the Nippon Seikokai (The Holy Catholic Church in Japan) in 1886. On his gravestone some Japanese friends placed this touching epitaph, "During his fifty years in Japan he taught Christ's ways and not his own."

John of Damascus

Died December 4, c.760

Priest and Monk

Champion of Orthodox Christianity

The son of an important official in the court of the Moslem Caliph of Damascus, John had an easy rapport with the Moslems among whom he was reared and whom he regarded as simply heretical Christians. He readily succeeded to his father's office in the Caliph's court. Later, he abandoned the wealth and comfort of the fashionable life of Damascus and joined a religious community in Palestine.

As he lived the rigorous life of a monk in the stark wilderness near the Dead Sea, his own rich and strong personality began to emerge. He soon distinguished himself as a theologian and scholar. His chief published work extant is *The Fount of Knowledge*. He is recognized as a "Doctor of the Universal Church." However, John of Damascus is most widely remembered for his contributions to Christian worship. He wrote many fine hymns, including two Easter ones that are still popular today: "Come ye faithful raise the strain . . ." and "The Day of Resurrection, earth tell it out abroad!" He effectively defended the doctrine of the Real Presence in the Eucharist, the veneration of the Lord's Mother, and use of sacred pictures, "icons." In the latter he became envolved in an international religio-political struggle called the "Iconoclastic Controversy" which reached violent proportions and shook the Byzantine world. His life was saved in this controversy by his powerful Moslem friends.

Clement of Alexandria
Died December 5, c.210

Priest

Early Scholar and Apologist

Titus Flavius Clement was a sophisticated Greek, well educated in philosophy and well traveled. He was converted to Christianity largely through the efforts of Pantaenus, the head of a Christian school in Alexandria, Egypt. Unlike some of his contemporaries, Clement was not at all willing to leave his philosophical training at the baptismal font. He found Christianity to be quite compatible with philosophy and he continued to practice and refine his speculative skills. He regarded Socrates and Plato as important forerunners of Christ, asserting that their teaching prepared men to accept and understand the gospel much as the Old Testament prophets had.

His extent works include: *An Exhortation to the Greeks* and *Instruction in Christian Living.* For most of his adult life his home was Alexandria, with its renowned library and university. Clement served as principal of the Christian school there. However, he also visited the Christian communities in Antioch and Jerusalem, where he was highly regarded. He died under unknown circumstances during the persecution of the Emperor Septimus Severus.

O God, who has enlightened your Church by the teaching of your servant Clement: Enrich us evermore, we beseech you, with your heavenly grace, and raise up faithful witnesses to the truth of your salvation.

Nicholas

Died December 6, c.342

Bishop of Myra

Protector of Children and Sailors

It is no wonder that in England, a country so concerned about her children and her navy, more churches have been named in honor of Nicholas than for any other saint. He was the Bishop of Myra in what is now Turkey.

Tradition has it that he was a nobleman who poured out his fortune to care for poor children. Countless legends surround his deeds of kindness to sailors. Dutch settlers in New Amsterdam called him "Santa Claus." His costume and his image have been secularized and his beloved ships have been replaced by, of all things, reindeer. But, his spirit of love for children remains.

Clement Clarke Moore, a devoted churchman and professor at the General Theological Seminary in New York, has left us a pleasant bit of fantasy called "A Visit From St. Nicholas" which begins, "Twas the night before Christmas. . . ." Around the world at Christmas time St. Nicholas will not be forgotten in song and ceremony, but those who honor him best are those who honor his Lord and who work continually for the care and protection of children.

Almighty and everlasting God, who did enkindle the flame of your love in the heart of your servant Nicholas: Grant to us, your humble servants, the same faith and power of love; that, as we rejoice in his triumph, we may profit by his example.

148

Ambrose

Bishop of Milan

A Father of the Western Church

Ambrose was born of a prominent and powerful Roman family and at the time he was acclaimed Bishop of Milan he was an important Roman official, but had not yet been baptised! He accepted the Christian faith and the office of bishop in virtually the same breath. He had been studying to become a Christian but on the day he was elected bishop he had entered the cathedral only as a ruler of state interested in quelling the violent conflict between the Arians and the orthodox Christians.

During the next quarter century he emerged as a great spokesman and organizer of the church. He became perhaps the most renowned preacher of his day and is credited with converting Augustine of Hippo. He was a highly competent scholar and theologian. He was a hymn writer of some distinction (see *The Hymnal 1940,* 132, 158, and 160). He contributed so much to the design of Christian worship in Milan the rite used there still bears his name, the Ambrosian Rite. He was diligent against heresy, but chastised fellow bishops who allowed heretics to be executed. He was fearless in contending with officials of the Roman state and once even excommunicated the emperor when the latter had perpetrated a vengeful massacre.

Grant to all bishops and pastors the same excellency in preaching and fidelity in ministering your Word as given to your servant Ambrose.

Thomas

Apostle

Poor Thomas has been saddled with the unhappy agnomen, "the Doubter," since the earliest days of the church. This is due, of course, to the account of him in the 20th chapter of John's Gospel. Countless sermons and many fruitful meditations have come out of the consideration of Thomas's doubts. It is significant that he was the namesake of Thomas Aquinas, the great questioner and teacher of the Middle Ages. Some have held that doubt is the antithesis of faith, others that it is the mother and nourisher of faith. Certainly there are many kinds and levels of doubting. Thomas's kind of doubting, his forthright, honest questioning, has made him an attractive and popular person to modern men who tend to see great virtue therein. It is interesting that "doubting" Thomas is the first of the apostles to proclaim our Lord's divinity after the resurrection.

Thomas was a twin. He was the alleged author of an apocraphal gospel. We do not know where he went after the resurrection or where he died, but traditions of his missionary activities are in evidence from Iran to the Malabar coast of India.

O Eternal God, who did strengthen your apostle Thomas, being doubtful, with firm and certain faith in the resurrection of your Son our Lord: Grant unto us your people, that we may be not faithless but believing, until we come to see our Savior in his glory face to face; through the same Son Jesus Christ our Lord.

The Nativity of our Lord Jesus Christ

The Light Shineth in Darkness

The historic date of Jesus' birth is unknown, but from the early days of the church this seemed a particularly appropriate time to remember the event. It is the period of the winter solstice, a dramatic and important natural phenomenon in much of Europe: the time when the days begin to lengthen and the light of the sun begins to stage its comeback. It was already the joyful feast of Saturnalia to the Romans. What better time to celebrate with gladness the coming of "The Light of the World"? (The second collect for Christmas Day and the Gospel lesson from John 1 carry out this theme.)

The gospel accounts of Matthew and Luke record the events surrounding Jesus' birth of Mary in Bethlehem, and although we are not given a date in the modern sense, Luke is about as explicit as any ancient historian when he writes that Jesus was born in the days of Caesar Augustus, when Cyrenius was governor of Syria. Since the days when these gospels were written, every generation has contributed to the rich fabric of Christmas tradition. Perhaps Christmas has been too embellished, so that the bold simplicity of the actual event is sometimes lost. Yet, even amid all the commercialization and cheap theatrics of a 20th century Christmas, it is still possible for families and churches to celebrate the joyful mystery of our Lord's birth, when "the Word was made flesh and dwelt among us."

Stephen

Deacon and Martyr

Stephen was a man "filled with the Holy Spirit," who was the first of seven deacons appointed by the Apostles in Jerusalem. He was a stirring preacher and was endowed with the gift of healing. His effective proselyting for Christianity brought down upon him the wrath of the powerful Sanhedrin. He had been preaching in a synagogue when an angry mob "stopped their ears" and seized him, dragging him out of the city where he was stoned as a "blasphemer." Stephen died confessing Christ and praying for his persecutors. He was the first Christian martyr.

Grant, O Father, that in all our sufferings here on earth in witness to your truth, we may follow the example of our Lord and of his first martyr Saint Stephen, and learn to love our enemies and forgive our persecutors; through Jesus Christ our Savior, who lives and reigns with you and the Holy Spirit, one God, in glory everlasting.

Lo! what a cloud of witnesses
Encompass us around!
Men once like us with suffering tried,
But now with glory crowned.

Let us, with zeal like theirs inspired,
Strive in the Christian race;
And, freed from every weight of sin,
Their holy footsteps trace.

Apostle and Evangelist

The companionship of youth—frank, strong, and hearty —is one of the great pleasures of most men's lives. Jesus was no exception. His closest circle of intimate companions included Peter and the brothers, James and John, all fishermen by trade. They seem to have been at times a right rowdy crew. Jesus referred to the brother as "Sons of Thunder." It seems particularly appropriate that during the festive season of Christmas we remember this group of friends and especially John, Jesus' closest friend.

John is called the "Beloved Disciple." It was John who reclined nearest to Jesus at the Last Supper and it was to John that Jesus, on the cross, committed the care of his mother. Peter and John seem to have remained life-long friends. Together they went to the Lord's tomb. They were together at Pentecost and participated together in the healing of the lame man at the Beautiful Gate of the Temple. Together they appeared before the Sanhedrin and together they went to lay their hands on those who had been baptised in Samaria.

John visited the island of Patmos, but his most significant work seems to have been done in Ephesus. The New Testament writings which bear his name were apparently compiled there. He is said to have died in Ephesus, quietly, in his sleep. Presumably the only one of the Twelve to die a peaceful and natural death.

Illumine us also with the brightness of your light.

The Holy Innocents

Infant Victims of Herod's Purge

Herod, who ruled Palestine at the time of Our Lord's birth, held a dubious claim to the throne and was, understandably, threatened by the rumor of the birth of a legitimate king of the Jews. Only a person completely unversed in human history would question the possibility of his committing the heinous crime mentioned in Holy Scripture, the slaughter of the male infants of Bethlehem. Ghastly as the murder of innocent babies sounds to Christian ears, it is not without parallel in the annals of history. The famous Jewish historian Josephus testifies to the fact that Herod was "a man of great barbarity towards everybody," and tells us of crimes so shocking and bloody as to make the killing of the Holy Innocents appear mild by comparison.

Bethlehem was a very small town, but there, on a day that shall live in infamy, her few boy babies under two years of age were mercilessly taken from their parents and slain. Jesus was nearly one of them. The church has always honored these innocent children who died as martyrs without ever having even heard the name of Jesus. They were, as Augustine of Hippo wrote, "buds, killed by the frost of persecution the moment they showed themselves."

Grant, most merciful Father, that, as we remember the slaughter of innocent babes by the order of a tyrant, when our Lord was born, so we may be firm to defend all helpless people from cruelty and oppression.

INDEX